THE

SPARK

THAT

SURVIVED

THE
SPARK
THAT
SURVIVED

A MEMOIR BY **MYRA LEWIS WILLIAMS**

AUTHOR OF **GREAT BALLS OF FIRE**

Deeds Publishing | Atlanta

Published by Deeds Publishing in Athens, GA
www.deedspublishing.com

Printed in The United States of America

Back cover photograph by Matt King

Library of Congress Cataloging-in-Publications DSata is available upon request.

ISBN 978-1-944193-16-4
EISBN 978-1-944193-17-1

Books are available in quantity for promotional or premium use. For information, email info@deedspublishing.com.

First Edition, 2016

10 9 8 7 6 5 4 3 2 1

CONTENTS

1. Goodbye, Levi! | 1957

It was a cold, overcast winter day in Memphis, Tennessee. The sky was as gray as my daddy's big wool topcoat. The winds were perfectly still. The lake showed no sign of life. No birds flew from tree-to-tree and no trees swayed. Everything seemed to be holding its breath. Nothing moved anywhere.

I could see the lake and its calm waters from my school bus window. The bus stopped in front of my house on East Shore Drive, as it had for years. I was the only one off at this stop and bounded down the steps, ran up the driveway, and turned and waved goodbye to the bus, like I always did. There were no warnings; no signs along the way indicated that this would be the last time I would be on this school bus. Nothing seemed out of the ordinary. If so, maybe I would have taken one last quick look back over my shoulder as my bus drove away.

Nothing was out of the ordinary, or so I thought. How could I know what awaited me in a few short hours? How could I know that I would never again ride the school bus or attend a day of class at Levi Elementary School? Whatever happened to the contents of my desk, I don't know. A jacket I may have left behind was most likely tossed away when they realized I really wasn't going to be back there… ever. I had my last meal that day in our noisy cafeteria and my last time talking to the nice cafeteria ladies. They liked me, mainly because I ate everything they cooked. I loved it all and drank all of my milk, as well as my non-milk-drinking classmates' milk.

It was simply a very normal day for me at school. No warning bells, no indication, no signs whatsoever that this day would firmly close, or I should say slam shut, a major chapter in my life. It would send me down a path that few have to navigate at my age.

It was plain; it was simple: This was the last day of my childhood. The last day of my formal education, the day I would surrender my childhood and step into a woman's place, in spite of being only thirteen years old. Something was about to take place that would not only change my life but the life of my family, something that would ultimately become known around the world. It would make front page scandalous headline news; it would destroy a career; it would tear our family apart like a bomb, leaving rubble in its path. Suffice it to say, it would break my daddy's and my momma's hearts. I would be accused of things I could have never dreamed of, such as it was all my idea! Pitied by some, disgusting to others, I was unprepared for any of it.

This would have been my last year at Levi. My classmates and I would be graduating from Levi Elementary School and starting a new phase of life—high school. It was a huge new world that I wasn't looking forward to. I had been at Levi since 4th grade; now I would be leaving this familiar place with its friendly cafeteria ladies, not knowing what to expect. The mere thought caused a lot of fear, but all of my worry was for naught, for I would never make it to Whitehaven High, not next year, not next century, not ever. Before the clock would strike midnight

I would stand beside my daddy's cousin Jerry Lee Lewis while a Baptist minister pronounced us "man and wife." I wore the same dress I wore to school. Jerry was unprepared and had *no* ring to slip on his new bride's finger. He just never thought about it. Wouldn't you think with all of the other preparation, a ring just might have come to mind? Ya think?

Jerry had been visiting his family in Louisiana for a few days and had returned to our house in Memphis, where he'd been living with my family. Shortly after I got home from school he asked me to come out to the car because he had something to show me. I followed him out the door and sat down in the front passenger seat of his old Ford. He reached past me and opened the glove box of his black and white Ford, and handed me a navy blue folder. I opened it and read the caption a couple of times just to make sure I was reading it right. In big bold letters across the top, it said MARRIAGE LICENSE...Jerry Lee Lewis and Myra Brown. I read it and turned to ask him a real stupid question.

"Are we married?" I thought you had to stand in front of some people and say something.

"No," he said, "but we are going to be. That's the license." He explained that he had called upon a friend to pose as me and sign my name to the Mississippi license in Natchez. She was twenty-five years old so they didn't ask for any identification.

I was dumbstruck.

"What are you saying?" I asked Jerry. "I'm thirteen years old and my Daddy will kill you!"

"No, he won't," Jerry insisted. "We've got a band together and he likes me."

"Let's just get married in a couple of years," I mumbled.

"Myra," he said, "I love you and I want to marry you."

"Okay," I said, "but in a couple of years, alright?"

My mind goes blank of what he said after that…I think he said, "It's now or never."

So with the clear logic of a child I made a decision that I should have never had to make. I did love Jerry and I was very mature for my age. But I was still only a kid.

We went back into the house, trying to act as normal as possible. Mom cooked supper, like always, and we all sat around the table laughing and talking as usual. Jerry got up from the table, stretched his arms, and with a big yawn asked if I would like to go to a movie with him.

"Can I, Mom?" I asked.

"Yes," she replied, "but you can't be out late; you've got school tomorrow."

"Okay," I said.

Out the door we went. Jerry drove out to Highway 61 and took Holmes Road south. The Mississippi state line was less than a mile or two from where we lived. I got the feeling Jerry knew exactly where he was going, as he probably found it before coming to our house that day. He turned into a driveway with a sign that read *Wedding Chapel*. We went inside and Jerry did the talking, asking a man if we could get married that night.

Two very sweet but elderly ladies stood over to the side and giggled. I had the feeling this was their only form of excitement.

"Can we decorate your car?" they asked, like two silly kids.

"Oh no!" we said. "You can't do that. Nobody knows we're getting married."

They had called the preacher and he arrived shortly after. My mind goes blank on the details after this but I think someone handed me a bouquet of flowers to hold. The next thing I recall was the sweet old ladies throwing rice at us as we went out the door. I do remember laughing. They had gone ahead and decorated the car with tin cans and "Just Married" written all over it.

But they decorated the wrong car. They decorated the preacher's car, not ours. If not, we would have been looking for a carwash. We jumped into Jerry's Ford and headed back home.

When we walked in, my daddy said, "I thought ya'll were going to a movie." We were taken by surprise, but came up with a good excuse: The movie wasn't any good. Thank goodness no one asked us the name of it.

We had been gone less than an hour.

Jerry had a habit of combing his hair and as he did so standing in the kitchen, rice fell all over the floor. I thought I was going to faint. I gave him a "get out of here" look. He took the clue, and went out in the backyard and shook the rest of the rice out of his hair. The rice had missed me; sometimes it pays to have a ponytail that you can shake.

Thus began my married life. It was many days before we told Momma and Daddy. That's when I got my first whoopin'. And just like I predicted, my daddy tried to kill Jerry Lee. Daddy went looking for him with a shotgun. Jerry had enough sense to leave town for a couple of weeks until his cousin, now his new father-in-law, calmed down.

So at age thirteen I was no longer Myra Gale Brown. I was Myra Gale Lewis. I did the only thing I knew to do. I emptied my doll suitcase, stuffed in my favorite jeans and jammies, and left my beloved parents' warm and loving home to go live my own married life. Little did I know it would be years before I would be able to have my own warm and loving home, and that it would be miles away from my husband Jerry Lee Lewis.

2. Skeletons in the Closet—and on the Porch | 1700s-1900s

My life story begins in 1756. Not mine exactly, of course, but the earliest stories I know about my ancestors on my daddy's side of the family. That's the year my forebear Jeremiah Lewis landed in North Carolina from Wales. There's a rumor he was running from the law, but we don't know for sure.

Thus begins the Lewis family saga. It's the side of my family I'm most familiar with because not only was I born into it, I married into it. Once you hear a few stories about my ancestors, my marriage at age thirteen to my second cousin will be less of a shock. Women marrying young and family marrying family were not new to this clan.

This family legacy also includes murder, music, religion, bootlegging, and general mayhem. An exemplary family this is not, but no one could ever accuse us of being dull.

Eventually, one arm of the family migrated west, landing in Louisiana. It was there two cousins; Leroy, known as Lee, and Arilla; married. Lee was a teenager when he visited his aunt just after she'd given birth to Arilla. He found his baby cousin to be so charming he declared right then and there that when she grew up he was going to marry her. And he did.

Arilla was fourteen in 1888 when she traveled to visit her aunt and uncle and their family. There was a square dance and her cousin Lee, by then thirty-two years old, apparently swept her off her feet. They married the very next day.

It's Arilla, my great-grandmother, who has stolen my heart and my admiration, even though we only met when I was so small I don't remember it. If she ever had a girl's dreams of a happy marriage and a cozy home with a white picket fence, no one knows. That certainly was not what she got. Her cousin and new husband Lee took her straight home to his cabin with the dirt floor, and began a non-stop stream of procreation for years to come.

By age thirty-six Arilla had eleven kids. Lee assisted in all of the deliveries at home. He sharecropped and she would have had nothing to do but work from dawn to dusk to take care of her brood.

Sometimes I sit and just think about this. No matter what has happened in my life, I've never had eleven children to feed and clothe. I can't even wrap my brain around that. Arilla must have been an amazingly strong woman. That strength, I feel, has been passed on, whether from tradition, storytelling, or DNA. I like to think that at least a sliver of Arilla's perseverance lives on in me. Knowing her story certainly makes me appreciate the life I have today.

Her daughter Jane was my grandmother and her son Elmo was the father of Jerry Lee Lewis. That's how my dad, J.W. Brown, Jane's son, and Jerry Lee Lewis, Elmo's son, are first cousins. And therefore Jerry Lee Lewis, my first husband, and I are second cousins.

So you can see with Arilla and Lee that the marriage of a young girl to an older cousin was not new to this family.

But there's so much more to the story of our clan that it's almost impossible to sort it all out. I'll do my best to hit a few highlights that are most meaningful to me. I think being aware of our heritage is important to understanding ourselves.

Arilla, my great-grandmother and Jerry's grandmother, had a hard life with Lee Lewis. It turns out he was a drinker and didn't make much money. He started out with a pharmacy business, which makes sense seeing that his father was a physician, but Lee somehow either lost or got out of the pharmacy business and ended up sharecrop farming.

Lee is remembered by many as having been rather mean. Amazingly, it seems that most of their offspring, save one, inherited Arilla's sweet nature and kindness.

Eventually their kids grew up and started marrying. Now this is where it really gets confusing. Just keep in mind that they lived in a small town and apparently finding a mate wasn't all that easy. There weren't that many to pick from.

Of the eleven Lewis children, four married Gilley siblings. Whether the town was out of eligible Gilleys or for other reasons, one Lewis sister married a Swaggart. Jane Lewis, my grandmother, broke the mold and married a Brown. They are my daddy's, J.W. Brown's, parents. (By the way, J.W. is his full name. It doesn't stand for anything else.) But it gets better. Elmo married Mamie Herron. Mamie had a sister who needed a husband, so that sister married a Swaggart. There was another Herron sister who married the most successful bootlegger in town, and he helped some of the Lewis and Swaggart men get into that business during Prohibition.

Got it? If not, don't worry about it. You get the gist. The same names keep popping up.

My daddy remembers being a kid and visiting his grandparents at the cabin. One time he and his brother were playing in the garden and Grandpa Lee chased them out with a big butcher knife. They never knew if he really was mad at them or just entertaining himself. They were afraid of him.

But Grandma Arilla was another story. They adored her. Five feet eight inches tall, with long legs and hazel eyes, her grandkids found her to be warm, fun, and loving. At barely five feet tall myself, I marvel at her height and wish that long leg gene had found its way to me.

In his seventies Lee got throat cancer. Arilla somehow scavenged enough money to send him to the doctor. But he stopped at a tavern on the way and never made it to the doctor. He died of cancer.

When the old man passed away the family prepared for a wake, a carry-over from Welsh Celtic tradition. Lee's body was laid out in the house, awaiting the celebration of his life. For those who lived there, the wait for the next day's event left plenty of time for drinking, which gave the youngest of the eleven children the opportunity to conjure up a joke to play on his older siblings. Only in the haze of booziness could this have seemed like a good idea. With the help of friends, he moved his father's body to a rocking chair on the front porch and tied it in place with twine. He even placed his dad's corn cob pipe in the corpse's lifeless hand. Then he attached twine to the rocker and hid in the bushes as family and friends arrived. Yanking on the string, he rocked the chair, snickering at the sight of guests being horrified by the dead man in a rocking chair on the front porch.

After Lee died Arilla moved from house to house, taking the bus to live with one of her children after another for a few months each visit. She died at age 97.

So that's a bit about the Lewis clan and the family tales that came down to me. We come from wild and wooly beginnings, to be sure. But if you think that's bad, I invite you to look into your own ancestry. I say that with a smile on my face, because I suspect all of us have some skeletons in our family closets. Most just don't put them on the porch.

Laying my life out there in this memoir feels a bit like putting my skeletons on the porch for all to see. Sometimes uncomfortable and sometimes a pleasure, it's been a daunting task. If you're a woman who has survived life's worst tragedies and your own dumbass decisions, like me, I hope this book will be a comfort to you.

Let's embrace Arilla as our guide. Like her, we can survive whatever life throws our way. We can come out stronger than ever before. We can support each other. We take whatever sparks we still hold inside and fan that flame to light up our lives together.

3. Rock-and-Roll Romance | 1942

In case you're still wondering how I could possibly have made the decision to sneak away and get married at such a tender age, let me tell you about my parents' marriage. You'll see that I had a teenager's dreams about wedded bliss because my parents had—and still have—a true Hollywood love story. Theirs is a fairytale romance that flourished in the era of rock-and-roll.

As their first child, I've heard their story so many times I can recite it in my sleep.

It goes beyond love at first sight; it is two souls whose destiny was to be together. Little did they know, and little did they care, where life would take them, as long as they were together. Nothing would ever be more important than their love for each other. It almost makes you believe they had been together in another lifetime; they were so made for each other.

It was a chance meeting in 1942. J.W. Brown was fifteen years old, playing stand-up bass in his family band "The Mississippi Hotshots." The band was comprised of his mother Jane, who played the piano; one brother Otis, who played fiddle and sang; the other brother Charles, who played mandolin; and a family friend Claudie, who played steel guitar. That night they were appearing at the American Legion Hall in the small country town of Winnsboro, Louisiana, which wasn't too far from the Brown hometown. The price of admission: fifty cents. While on stage J.W. spotted a dark-eyed beauty as she was swept across the dance floor by her dancing partner.

J.W. swears that at the very moment he saw Lois, he said to himself, "Now there's the girl for me." Later on that week, while driving, J.W. saw the guy that was dancing with "his girl" and tried his best to run him off the road. I am certain this poor guy had no idea why somebody was acting like a deranged madman trying to run him into the ditch!

"After all," I said to Daddy years later, "that was his girl, *not* yours. He should have run *you* off the road." Daddy would just laugh and snicker at me. He had found his "true love and it was just a matter of time." He had a lot of tricks up his sleeve and he was quite willing to use them all.

Lois' Papa wasn't as fond of J.W. as J.W. would have liked. However, J.W. didn't think running Lois' Papa off the road would be the best way to handle him. He quickly learned that everybody in town knew that if you were going to be anywhere near Lois, first you would have to be approved by her Papa Neal.

But J.W. was an entertainer who had been a musician on stage ever since he was a kid, so he figured he'd "entertain Papa" with no problem.

J.W. decided a phone call would be a good way to start. He reached for the phone and confidently dialed the number.

Lois answered, with Papa in hearing distance watching every move over the rim of his glasses. J.W.'s first comment was, "Ask your Papa, would he like to go fishing?"

Lois repeated it word-for-word: "Papa, J.W. said, 'Would you like to go fishing?'"

"Hell no," Papa replied. "I don't want to go fishing."

13

"'Hell no,'" Lois repeats from her Papa back to J.W. "He doesn't want to go fishing."

J.W. comes back with, "Well, ask him if he would like to go huntin'."

Once again Lois repeats the message. "Papa, J.W. said, 'Would you like to go huntin'?'"

Once again, her Papa said, "Hell no! I don't want to go huntin'."

Not to be defeated, J.W. gives it one more shot. "Lois," he says, "ask your Papa what he likes to do."

"Papa," said Lois, in a little sing-song voice. "J.W. said for me to ask you, 'What do you like to do?'"

Papa pushed his glasses back on to his nose, looked straight at his daughter, and said "Tell him I like to stay home and mind my own damn business."

This wasn't going exactly as J.W. had planned and he was a little caught off guard. Without hesitating he said, "Well tell your Papa I said 'go to hell.'"

Lois did as she was told. "Papa, J.W. said 'go to hell.'"

The next sound J.W. heard was a long-winded dial tone.

J.W. thought to himself, "There's more than one way to skin a cat."

The next day Lois came home from school, and turning the corner she spotted her Papa and J.W. Brown sitting on the front porch laughing, talking, and drinking beer. For fear of "what was going on" she sprinted up the porch steps two at a time and flew into the house, letting the screen door slam behind her.

J.W. had figured that if hunting and fishing don't appeal to a man, he's got to have something he enjoys. Turned out a half dozen bottles of cold beer was it. Especially if a man's wife won't let him drink in the house. "Porch beer" has got to hit the spot. Just how J.W. was able to hit the nail on the head is anybody's guess.

"Young lady," Papa called out, "where's your manners? Don't you see you've got company?"

Lois had visions of her mother, Roxie, marching onto the porch and confiscating their beer, so Lois approached her mother cautiously. Roxie looked up at her daughter and said, "Sweetie your daddy and J.W. are on the porch. Why don't you go out and join them?"

Confused, Lois thought to herself, "There's something going on around here!"

What was going on was that J.W. Brown had been welcomed with open arms from that first night on the porch with Papa. And Roxie loved J.W. almost as much as she loved her own kids. Instead of losing a daughter they had gained a son. As long as Oscar and Roxie Neal lived there was never a cross word between them and their son-in-law.

That J.W. was some kind of charmer. Smart, too. It didn't take him long to figure out that if fishing and hunting wouldn't work, beer just might. And it did.

It was a beautiful September day in 1943 when Papa proudly gave the bride away. Lois wore a beautiful blue dress bought by her Papa for this special occasion. The groom wore a white dress shirt and a pair of dress pants, his tie in his pocket.

They were both sixteen years old. They were considered to be "kids" and maybe they were, but they were also certain, absolutely certain, of what they wanted from life. They knew this was the love of their life, and they reached out with both hands and embraced it with everything they had and gave it their all. They were in love with each other and still are.

Now wouldn't you think that when their daughter got married a little young that they would have remembered this….but no-o-o-o-o. For their daughter to marry at thirteen to a man twenty-two didn't set too well with either one of them. There were no warm fuzzy feelings here. I was their only daughter and too young. It made my Daddy fighting mad that his own cousin had talked me into running away with him to get married, and we had to keep distance between the two men for a while.

My dad was, naturally, protective of me. I wish every kid could have parents who love each other as much as mine. That love brushed off on my younger brother Rusty and me. There was never any doubt in our house that we were safe and secure and adored.

So when I was thirteen years old I'd never seen anything of marriage other than mutual respect, adorable adoration, and unending love. That's what I expected of my own marriage.

Oh the storybook dreams of a child.

4. The Electrocution | 1956

In 1950 a Memphis newspaper was inadvertently tossed onto my grandparents' porch. Grandmother Neal asked my daddy if he'd like to see it. Now a family man with a small daughter, J.W. had been looking for better work than being a lineman in their small town. So he took the paper and immediately went to the want ads, where he saw that Memphis Light Gas and Water was hiring linemen. This would be a bigger company with better pay than what he was used to.

You see, J.W. Brown had always had a dream of being able to support his family in style. The picture he had in his head harkened back to one day when he was just a kid. He and his brother were walking down a country road when a man in a big, shiny, new Cadillac car drove up and stopped. He asked the boys to open a gate for him. They did and he gave each of them a nickel. When that man drove through the gate and on down the lane J.W. said, "Someday I'm gonna get me one of those cars." Working for a small company in a small town, he had yet to get his Cadillac car.

The very next day after the newspaper hit the porch, he made the five-hour drive to Memphis, parked in front of the building of MLG&W, walked in, and applied for the job. He was hired on the spot after they learned he had six years of experience.

No one ever found out who left that newspaper on my grandparent's porch, but it changed everything.

After working a week J.W. returned to Winnsboro, Louisiana, where we lived, and packed up his little family, my mom and me. Everybody said their goodbyes and we headed north on Highway 61 to Memphis. But at five years old, all I knew was that Memphis was 250 miles away from Mommaw, my Grandma Neal. I cried the entire 250 miles. I wanted to stay with my Mommaw. "I hate Memphis" I said, "and I don't want to go!" I cried to no avail.

My daddy loves to tell about how after being hired he walked to his car, paused, and looked west down the street thinking to himself, "This is home now; this is home." He was looking forward to a new start, a new job, and working for a company where he could someday retire. Yes, this will be a good move, he thought.

Fate had another plan. Memphis Light Gas &Water put him to work, then put him in the hospital, and then put him in show business.

You see, the offices of MLG&W were located on Union Avenue. A block down across the street was a small recording studio owned by Sam C. Phillips. It had opened January, 1950, and was known as "Memphis Recording Services." One day that sign would come down and in its place would be a round yellow sign that read "Sun Records."

My daddy had no idea how important that sign would become in his life. It all started on a day like any other work day with MLG&W. The crew daddy worked with drove to their assigned site for the day at Union Avenue Extension. The plan was to replace worn out wires on a sixty-foot pole. In those days there were no lifts with big metal baskets, like the "cherry pickers" we see today. Those didn't exist in the

'50s. The men actually climbed the poles using their boots that had spikes on the soles.

By then Daddy had worked for MLG&W for seven years. He'd lost friends on the job, either because their luck ran out or they were careless. He was never careless, but his luck was about to run out. There was a superstition that a lineman's life was ten years and this was Daddy's thirteenth year as a lineman. It was an unlucky year, to be sure.

Daddy hooked his safety belt and dug his spiked boots into the pole as he climbed to the top. He reached for the old wire, but in a flash it slithered out of its cover and like an angered serpent it struck. First it set Daddy's shirt on fire; on the second strike it hit his left arm as he tried to fight it off, with the voltage coming out of the palm of his left hand and left foot. Unbelievably, the current never crossed his body. If it had, he would have been killed instantly.

J.W. remembers knowing that his pole buddies were coming for him, but the pain was unbearable. He just hoped he could hang on before falling to his death.

The next sound he heard was his wife's screaming as she entered the ER at the hospital. She'd seen his boots outside the door and thought that meant he'd died, seeing that a dead man's boots are always removed.

Old tradition was to remove a man's boots when he died because the feet would swell and leather boots would have to be cut off with a knife. There was no reason to ruin a good pair of boots.

The company gave J.W. a year to heal with full pay, with an offer of a desk job after that. But he knew he was done. At age thirty, he'd climbed his last pole and wanted nothing more to do with electricity.

That meant he had to find work. The only other thing he knew how to do was play bass in a band. But he needed a band. That's when he went home to Louisiana seeking his younger cousin that he kept hearing about from other family members. They said this Jerry Lee Lewis, who Daddy hadn't seen since he was a little kid, could really play a piano.

So, as you can see, it was my daddy who brought Jerry Lee Lewis into our lives. I've always teased Daddy that it was his fault that I ever met Jerry in the first place.

Of course, none of us had any idea where that first meeting would lead. How could we ever have imagined such a thing?

5. **Hello, Jerry!** | 1956

After months of healing after being electrocuted on the job, J.W. Brown went in pursuit of his younger first cousin, Jerry Lee Lewis. Jerry was an unknown musician working in a small beer joint, the Hilltop Nightclub, in Natchez, Mississippi. Daddy knew the Hilltop well. He'd played in a band there when he was fourteen years old, the same year he and his brother had a weekly Saturday afternoon radio show there. Natchez, with its beautiful old antebellum homes, wasn't a big city but it was a lot bigger than the backwoods towns most Lewis' grew up in. With the highway coming straight down from Ferriday, Louisiana, to Natchez, Mississippi, it seemed as if this Jerry Lee Lewis was tracing J.W. Brown's tracks.

When my daddy's grandmother, Arilla Lewis, found out that he was looking for his cousin Jerry Lee Lewis, she told Daddy, "That boy will ruin your life." Arilla had lived with her son Elmo, his wife Mamie, and their family, so knew firsthand what their son Jerry Lee was like. In her eighties and widowed, Arilla no longer had a home of her own. She'd travel from one of her eleven children's homes to another. Whenever she stayed with Elmo and his family her time there was not good. Mamie apparently wasn't pleased with having her mother-in-law in the house. Even though some in the family believed that Jerry Lee had been terribly spoiled by his mother Mamie, my daddy had also heard about Jerry Lee's amazing musical ability.

So we will never know exactly what Arilla meant by her statement because, even though he adored his grandmother, J.W. ignored her warning and continued to follow his dream of getting back into the show business that he loved. Whatever it may be, he would endure it. Having a band with a talented cousin was the ticket to his dreams. With this Jerry's talent, and his own drive and determination to succeed, my daddy thought, "What could possibly be so bad?"

He should have listened to his grandmother.

When Daddy found him Jerry was playing drums while a blind man named Paul played the piano. I know that seems odd seeing that Jerry is famous for his piano playing. But he can play just about any musical instrument: guitar, fiddle, drums, piano. The Hilltop had needed a drummer, so that's what he was doing. Jerry's take-home pay wasn't enough to afford a roof over his head so, although twenty-one years old and married, he lived with his mother, father, and two younger sisters.

Before the night was over Jerry did play the piano to demonstrate his unique style. Daddy begged him to go back to Memphis with him, offering promises of an audition with Sam Phillips of Sun Records and a place to stay until the audition took place. Daddy had just heard enough to know that Jerry Lee Lewis would be a force to be reckoned with in the music business. There was nobody like him out there.

Jerry wasn't impressed with his cousin's offer and turned it down flat. After all, he and his dad Elmo had once saved all of their money from selling eggs, had gone to Sun Records in Memphis, and the place had been closed. They never got in. With no more eggs to sell and no more money, they went on home.

To top off Jerry's refusal, when Daddy and Jerry went out into the parking lot the hood of Daddy's Cadillac was standing straight up, wide open. Somebody in this rowdy part of town had tried to take his battery, unsuccessfully.

But Daddy wasn't about to give up on Jerry, so writing his address and phone number on a scrap of paper, he folded it up and pressed it into Jerry's hand, leaving the invitation open just in case Jerry had a change of heart.

From that moment on another force took over and directed the lives of those that would play a part in this event...this event that would be a total life-changer.

Daddy had been home from Natchez less than two days when our phone rang and I answered. It was someone calling from a phone booth, asking for directions to our house. "Daddy," I said, somewhat puzzled, "it's a man wantin' to get directions to our house."

Daddy grabbed the heavy black receiver from my hand and spoke firmly into the mouthpiece, "Where are you, Jerry? I'll be right there."

I seldom hear anyone mention that it was my daddy who got Jerry started on his career by inviting Jerry to come to Memphis and by arranging that first meeting at Sun Records. For months my parents, J.W. and Lois Brown, welcomed Jerry into our home, fed him, and encouraged him at every turn. All of this with not so much as a loaf of bread being offered in return. But that was okay, as far as my parents were concerned. Jerry's talent was undeniable and my daddy was a great bass player. Together in a band they couldn't help but make it. At least that was the attitude they had—and, obviously, it eventually worked.

That fateful night when Jerry called and Daddy took off

to fetch him, I went back to finish my 7th grade arithmetic homework at the dining room table. Daddy returned in record time with a stranger in tow, a funny looking guy wearing a red plaid shirt, jeans, cowboy boots, and sporting a way too short haircut as his ears stuck straight out. When the stranger smiled, one front tooth was smaller than the other, which almost made this twelve-year-old laugh out loud. So I went back to finish my arithmetic.

The adults talked and talked while I ignored them. Then I heard something that made me lose my concentration and my desire to finish that stupid homework. Jerry had sat down at our piano and was pounding out a boogie woogie as I had never witnessed before. I now knew how Alice felt as she fell down the rabbit hole. At that moment I knew our lives were about to change and nothing would ever go back to the way it was before. Nothing could possibly ever be the same again.

I didn't know, of course, how true that would turn out to be. I didn't know that the first time my parents and I went to one of his concerts Jerry would look right at me while he was performing and without my parents noticing he would mouth the words, "I love you."

I didn't know that I, too, was going to fall in love right back.

When Jerry and I secretly married, I had no idea what pain and sorrow I would be causing my family. I discovered that love does not necessarily conquer all.

6. The "Honeymoon" | 1957

For the next few days after my secret wedding I walked around like a deer caught in headlights. I felt as if I were going to explode from the pressure of knowing I had to tell my parents and the fear of what they were going to do.

So I took a scared kid's way out. One day I just left the marriage license out on my dresser for the world to see. Naturally our maid, Josie Mae, found it and went running to my parents, as I knew she would.

Was I ever glad I missed that scene! I'd left the house but knew I'd have to go home and face them knowing they most likely knew. When I walked in my daddy started taking off his leather belt. Now this was a bad omen. I'd never had a whipping before. My mother got between us and fought a good fight but Daddy did get one good swing at me that made contact with my rear end. Mom finally convinced him this would do no good.

I think Daddy agreed because he stopped and got out his trusty handgun, a .22 pistol. He stomped out to his car and drove away.

My mother and I both knew where he was going. She grabbed the phone and got Sam Phillips on the line.

"Get Jerry out of town!" she shouted. "J.W. is going to kill him if you don't! He's done married Myra!"

Jerry was right there with Sam, and later Jerry told me Sam grabbed him by the arm and said, "Well, you've done it now! Get yourself out of town if you want to see the sun rise tomorrow. J.W. is on his way here to shoot your dumb ass!"

Jerry sprinted out the door to his car and quickly drove to the airport. He took the next flight leaving regardless of where it was going. Nobody ever knew where he went. I'm not sure he knew.

Daddy arrived at Sun and Sam was ready for him. "Come on in J.W. and have a drink," Sam said.

Daddy replied, "I don't want no damn drink. I just want to shoot that kinky-headed bastard. Where is he?"

As is evident today, Sam talked Daddy out of killing his cousin and new son-in-law, Jerry Lee Lewis.

Who knows what Sam said? Knowing him I can imagine he used reason and logic, telling my daddy that those two may have been destined to love each other and be together, and no one can take on the responsibility of changing those kinds of decisions.

Daddy didn't like it but in light of cold, hard reality the only thing he could do came with major consequences. Once it was started there would be no turning back; the law would be in charge, not my parents. If Jerry was turned in to the police, he would go to prison, his career would go out the window, and he and I would still be married.

The final comment Sam made was, "J.W., who's to say this is not their destiny and the love of their lives?"

Daddy made the gut-wrenching decision that the price was too high. Besides, he remembered how he had met the love of his life at sixteen. He finished his drink, bid Sam goodbye, got in his car, and drove home.

When he got there he told Mom to pack, that the next day they were leaving for New York City where the band was to appear at the Brooklyn Paramount Theatre for two weeks. He didn't speak to me.

It was December 15, 1957. When they drove away I cried and cried until I could cry no more. The hurt I had caused my parents broke my heart and there was nothing on this earth I could do now to change it. At that moment I would have gladly given my life, that marriage, to undo all that had been done in the past week.

If only life came with those options. I knew I had to be strong and mature. I had to make it work, for the pain this had caused. By all that was sacred, it was going to work....

7. **The Paramount Theatre** | 1957

Jerry and I, along with Russ, the drummer, drove to New York City from Memphis a few days after my parents learned about my marriage to Jerry. It was an uneventful but long, long journey.

This is when I packed my belongings in my "doll case" since my parents had left early for New York and I had always had my things packed in my mother's suitcase. I didn't have a suitcase of my own. This is where a misunderstanding later arose about me packing my belongings in a "dollhouse," as it was reported. It was actually a red hatbox style case that originally held my dolls' clothes, which is what it was made to be. So it was my dolls' suitcase, but it didn't scream dollhouse.

I was still agonizing over the hurt I had caused my parents. All through the drive Jerry never said a word about my parent's reaction. If he had any feelings one way or the other, I never heard it. As soon as we checked into the Manhattan Hotel at Times Square, Jerry dressed and left to do the first show at the Paramount Theatre in Brooklyn.

It was opening night for Jerry and the band. This would also be the first meeting between Jerry and Daddy since Daddy had gone after Jerry with his pistol. No one knew what to expect. The two of them could have had a fist fight right there on stage. It was a big night for Jerry's career, with the show being packed with headliners like Fats Domino and Buddy Holly.

I wasn't allowed to go to the Paramount—I was to stay hidden away in the hotel room—and I've always wished I could have seen what happened on that stage. The parts that were public were all over the newspapers, so I've been able to picture what the performance was like. But Jerry had to tell me what happened in private between him and my daddy.

My daddy J.W. and the drummer Russ had taken their places on stage and were warming up the audience when Jerry made his entrance. The crowd roared as they came out of their seats. Jerry gave the audience a friendly salute and they screamed even louder. In the midst of all of that uproar, J.W.'s and Jerry's eyes met. The audience was on their feet stomping and screaming: "Jer-ry, Jer-ry, Jer-ry…!" Jerry strolled over to Daddy, and the two men looked each other in the eye and shook hands. Then Jerry calmly meandered over to the piano and struck the keys as he went into the opening song without even sitting down.

The crowd had no idea what they had just witnessed. I wish I could have seen it; maybe I would have felt more assured about our future. But I never set foot inside the Paramount Theatre for the whole two weeks we were there. No one knew I existed except for the three men on stage and my mother.

A lot was at stake. It was at last dawning on me what a problem Jerry and I had created. It made me wonder just how long this juggling act could last. This, I realized, is what happens when you have a "surprise wedding," and you're too young and too stupid to realize the consequences. There had been no consideration given to anyone or anything and no thoughts of the future. There had been no time to think.

During the daytime when Jerry, Daddy, and Mom were

at the Paramount for a matinee, I would wander out onto the streets of the big city and just walk around. I'd never seen anything like New York City before and was agog with amazement.

One day I spotted a movie theater and bought a ticket to this horribly scary movie. I'll never forget it. The opening scene was foggy and creepy. They were dragging a lake for a dead body. They found it and pulled it into the boat. The camera focused on the face of the dead person and this big, dead eye stared *right at me*. I jumped up and ran out of the theater. It scared me to death! The very next day, however, I bought another ticket to that same movie and tried once again to watch this horrible film. It didn't work. The same thing happened. I ended up running out of the theater again when that scene came on. Believe it or not, on another day I tried a third time. Nope. I couldn't do it. I ran out again. That scary movie was really scary! To this day I have not watched that movie.

Years later I figured out why I would do such a thing. I was trying to face my fears. I was trying to be brave.

I was trying to grow up.

This was how my married life to Jerry Lee Lewis began.

Oh yeah, we really knew what we were doing.

8. **Signs of the Times** | 1957

Today when I do book signings and give presentations, I know that the elephant in the room is the topic of sex. People who come to my signings, who are mostly around my age, are too polite to ask but I know they're wondering about a thirteen-year-old girl having sex. They wonder if Jerry and I had already had sex when we got married, and if because of that I already felt like I "belonged" to him, as teenage girls do in those situations. Or, they wonder if Jerry and I were anxious to have sex but believed we had to be married first. After all, religious beliefs were stronger in those days and most people thought it was a sin to have sex without being married. A person would be damned to hell forever for such a thing.

Of course, we all know that today in the media talking openly about sex is as common as corn. People don't hesitate to bare all—literally. We've all overheard and seen more about other people's sex lives than we ever cared to know.

My response to the elephant is: I don't talk about sex. Call me old fashioned but in my mind that's private, something between two people. In other words, it's nobody else's damned business.

I will say that annulment or divorce, for any woman in general, wasn't considered the way it is today because once a woman married and shared sex with one man she was considered to be "damaged goods," if you will, in terms of ever being with another man.

I'm also sometimes asked about the law back then. "Wasn't it illegal for Jerry to marry a minor?" someone will ask. Believe it or not, it was legal in some states, especially Southern states, for a thirteen-year-old girl to marry without her parents' consent. It was illegal in Tennessee, where we lived, but was legal just over the state line in Mississippi. That's where Jerry took me for our ceremony. He'd planned it all out so that it would be legal. I, of course, had no clue about those kinds of things. Jerry could have been taken to court because he moved me across a state line and away from my residence for the ceremony, but that was a wrangle my parents decided not to get tied up in. They figured it wouldn't have made a difference and the truth is it wouldn't have. I would still have wanted to be with my husband and I would have been alienated from the family I dearly loved.

Today a thirteen-year-old girl getting married without a parent's consent wouldn't happen in any state in this country. Unfortunately, it's still legal in some other countries around the world. I know what it's like for girls who suddenly find themselves in an adult relationship and my heart goes out to them. I only hope they have loving family around them like I did, or at least some kind of support from their community. Although I was afraid to tell my parents everything that was going on in my marriage—because I didn't understand it all myself—once my dad calmed down and put his gun away, at least I had them nearby.

How fortunate I feel that they're still close, living just twenty miles from my house. I am blessed, to be sure. My relationship with them endured. That's more than I can say for my marriage.

9. **3+13=16** | 1958

My red Cadillac was the most beautiful car in the world. Jerry bought it for me soon after we got married and I loved driving my own fancy car. Of course, at age thirteen I could hardly see over the dashboard, and there was the pesky problem of not being old enough to have a driver's license, but I wasn't about to let that stop me.

After all, I had a wife's duties to perform like grocery shopping, banking, and going to the cleaners. From my perspective, I had to drive.

This caused a bit of chaos from time to time, like the time a police officer came into the bank while I was depositing stacks of cash from Jerry's shows. Jerry only accepted cash payments because a promoter once gave him a check that bounced. Ever since then it was cash only, so Jerry or Cecil, his agent, would end up carrying around a suitcase full of cash no matter where in the world they performed. They'd bring that suitcase home and I'd take it to the bank. Jerry never had anything to do with the banking. That was a wife's job.

So one day I was in the bank with my suitcase full of cash when the officer came in and asked who was driving that big, red Cadillac parked out front. An expensive new car in his territory brought immediate suspicion.

Panic-stricken because I didn't have a driver's license, I looked pleadingly at the teller, a nice woman I'd come to know during all of my trips to the bank with my piles of money.

She lied like a pro. "I am. I'm driving the Cadillac."

The policeman looked doubtful, like he knew something was fishy here, but he left it alone. Thank goodness he didn't notice the suitcase full of money or I'm sure he would have had questions about that, too.

Another day I was turning into the cleaners when a car started backing up in front of me. Then it rolled the other way. I looked to try to figure out what was going on and was floored to see the top of a tiny little head in the driver's window. It looked like a child was in the car while it was rolling back and forth in a small dip in the road. Then suddenly the car came back and hit my Cadillac before I could move.

It turned out that the little boy's mother was in the cleaners and had left him in the car. But he'd shifted the vehicle out of park and the rolling began.

When a policeman arrived he commented that the three-year-old child was not old enough to drive. Then he scolded me about not being old enough to drive, either.

However, the local newspaper reported the incident and noted that together we were old enough to drive.

Sometimes it just takes two to get a job done.

10. A Red Cadillac and a Hundred-Dollar Bill | 1958

Shortly before we married, Jerry's song *Whole Lotta Shakin' Going On* hit the top of the charts and we were on our way to the big time. Therefore, after we were married we had some money and bought a little house in Memphis, and I took to housekeeping and supporting my now famous husband in our own little brick cottage on Dianne Drive in the suburbs. We got the house in February after being married in December. It had two bedrooms, one and a half baths, a den, a living room with a picture window, an eat-in kitchen, and a single carport where a lone washing machine sat in a utility room. There was a clothesline in the backyard. I could see that there would be fragrant white gardenias blooming by the front door in the spring. It was the home of my dreams.

My mom drove me to Haverty's furniture store and helped me pick out all of the furniture in one single day: a sectional sofa, beds, tables, chairs, and furnishings for every room. When we were done at that store we went straight over to Sears for linens, cookware, a black-and-white TV (no such thing as color TV), a set of Melmac dishes, pillows, blankets, and a broom. One day it was an empty house, the next day it was a ready-to-be-lived-in home. My colors were pink with a touch of black thrown in. After all, it was the '50s.

Sometimes I'd leave my cozy cottage and go on tour with Jerry and the band.

One day on tour I was dragging, I was so tired. I could have slept twenty-four hours nonstop and prayed somebody would let me. I'd been on the road for what seemed like a month, but in reality it was only a few weeks. Jerry and the band dropped me off at an airport so I could fly home and get some well needed rest. I don't remember what time the flight left but I know it arrived in Memphis after midnight. I'd left my car at the airport when I flew out to join the tour, so I had a way home. The Memphis airport was no bigger than the lobby of a small hotel and from the front door I could see my red Cadillac parked right where I left it. I grabbed my suitcase and threw it in the back seat, so thankful I was only fifteen minutes from our house on Dianne Drive. Sleep, wonderful sleep, was soon to be mine, in my own bed. I fully intended to leave my suitcase in the car, and run and dive headfirst into that bed.

But that feeling went away when I pulled into the driveway.

It was pitch black inside and outside the house. The place was never locked. I'm not sure we even had a key to any door. It was a very different world in the 50's; no one I knew ever locked their house.

Alone there for the first time, I was afraid to go into that creepy dark house, which until then had been my comfy little reprieve. I sat in the driveway for a few minutes, mulling over this latest development. I knew one of my options was not going to happen and that was going into this dark house alone.

Decision made, I put my car in reverse, backed out of the driveway and headed for a motel. My search would take me all the way to Union Avenue downtown before I saw anything that looked like a motel or hotel. I parked right by the front door, went in the lobby, and signed and paid for a room for one for one night, or what was left of the night. I grabbed my suitcase and dragged myself inside where I fell face first onto the nearest bed. Sleep at last! Or that's what I thought until I realized I had not had anything to eat since lunch. I was starving. My growling tummy wouldn't allow slumber.

Oh Lord, that night was turning into a nightmare. When was it going to end? I knew there was a Huddle House a few blocks away as I'd driven past it, so I found my wallet and my car keys and headed back the way I came until I reached the bright lights of this all-night diner.

Jerry had handed me a hundred-dollar bill at the airport earlier that day and I had one quarter in my change purse. As I looked over the menu I worried about that big bill. Would they take it? So when the waitress asked for my order I confessed my dilemma.

As she walked away she said, "Hold on. Let me see what I can do." She came back and said, "No problem," and asked what I would like.

"Bacon and eggs," I said, "and a Coke, please!"

At least one thing was going in my favor. The food was great. When I was done eating, I could have laid my head down on their counter and gone to sleep right then. When the waitress told me my meal was free because they could not, after all, break a hundred dollar bill, I was so grateful. I left her my quarter as a tip. It was, after all, the most I could do.

I wished a million times that night that I'd gone into my little house on Dianne Drive and fought all of the demons waiting there for me. They couldn't possibly be as bad as what I would encounter before that dreaded night would end.

Unbeknownst to me, earlier that day while I sat quietly at the airport 500 miles from Memphis, someone in Memphis was hell-bent on robbing a bank. They had a plan, a gun, and a female driver in a red Cadillac. The thieves fled with a sack of hundred dollar bills. They made a successful grab and no one had seen them since, not until I showed up driving an exact same car and trying to buy breakfast with a hundred-dollar bill in the middle of the night.

It turned out that the Huddle House manager had called the police, who had asked him to keep me there until they could arrive. That was why I got a free breakfast.

The Memphis police had a big tip and they thought they were closing in on this lawless gang.

"It'll be a long time before they rob another bank and you can be assured they won't do it in Memphis, Tennessee, when we are finished with them," the Memphis police no doubt thought to themselves as their excitement built.

When I turned into the parking lot of the motel I was immediately surrounded by what seemed to be a hundred police officers with guns drawn and spotlights blinding me every way I turned. All I envisioned was me sitting in jail... for not having a driver's license! (I wasn't old enough to drive.) The police captain came over to my car, leaned in, and took a good look at me. Something told him I was not who they had originally thought.

He turned his flashlight off and softly said, "Who are you, little girl, and how old are you?"

I answered the last question first, "I'm thirteen years old and I'm married to Jerry Lee Lewis."

"What brings you downtown tonight?" the captain asked.

I looked him straight in the eye and said, "The boogie man under my bed." I knew better than to lie to a policeman.

By this time his officers had searched my room where they found my plane ticket, which corroborated my statement that I was in another state when this robbery took place. The captain apologized for bothering me and advised me to go home, as I wasn't in the best part of the city.

I watched as they drove away and sat quietly for a few minutes, enjoying the feeling of relief. I went into my motel room, grabbed my luggage, got in my car, and headed for Dianne Drive. The sun was about to come up and if I could live through this day and night I should be able to take on any boogie man out there.

11. **Many Squash, Oklahoma** | 1958

Going on tour with Jerry and the band vacillated between
being a barrel of laughs to being a bad nightmare. A typical
tour would last three to six weeks with one day off for rest,
whether we needed it or not. Each "gig," as they were called,
would be 250 to 500 miles apart. Traveling was by car. My
assigned seat was the backseat center position. It was the
most uncomfortable position in the entire car, except of
course for the trunk and trailer that housed the suits and
instruments.

There were few turnpikes, as interstate highways were
originally called, in the mid-1950s. Most of the roads were
two lanes, one north and one south. We whizzed by every
town square, giving towns names as we went by, like Long
Gone, Iowa, and Many Squash, Oklahoma.

I could make it for five or six days but longer than that
and my eyes were crossed from getting up early to ride and
staying up late for the show. I longed for the comfort of our
little house on Dianne Drive. I would have hitchhiked to
the next town just for a decent night's sleep.

These guys could go only so long before they would
commence to entertain themselves. Don't think for one
moment, as grueling as it was, that they didn't have fun on
the road.

Finding a decent meal was always a challenge, anyway,
so restaurants were a favorite place to goof around. For example, the drummer, Russ, would walk into a café behind

us tapping his walking stick quickly, right to left, right to left, on the floor as if he were blind as a bat. He'd talk real loud and other diners would stop to see what was happening. Once he had their attention, the show would begin. One of the band members would run over to help him to the table. Russ would resist and attempt to wallop the guy with his cane, missing with every swing, of course. At the table Russ would loudly disagree with what he should order as we all gave him suggestions from the menu, all of us speaking at the same time. These musicians were playing the audience like a fiddle. As we left, Russ would yell, "It's my turn to drive!" Several of us would protest, saying we were never going to let him drive *again*.

We thought these performances rivaled those of Hollywood. When piled back into the car, we laughed until our sides hurt. We'd been bored, that's all. So much so I was pleased they hadn't set the place on fire just to "amaze the audience."

12. **Unlucky 13** | 1958

I didn't mean to cause a culture shock to the world and destroy a career. Really, I didn't.

But that's what happened when Jerry did his first big tour overseas to cap his huge hits like *Great Balls of Fire* and *Whole Lotta Shakin' Going On*. Unluckily for his career, he took his thirteen-year-old bride with him.

It was a bunch of us that went to England including Jerry, his agent Oscar, the drummer Russ, my mom and dad Lois and J.W. Brown, Jerry's sister Frankie Jean, and my three-year-old brother Rusty. Jerry had wanted his parents to come, too, but they'd never flown on a plane and weren't about to start now.

To kick-off the tour before leaving the states, Jud Phillips from Sun Records arranged for Jerry to be on the *Dick Clark Saturday Night Beechnut Show*. Then I remember Jud and Jerry having an argument about me. It was hard to imagine anybody fighting about me, but there they were doing it.

It wasn't that Jud didn't seem to like me. He just thought that our six-month marriage needed to be kept secret, something we'd done well to that point. Jud didn't want Jerry to talk about me or to take me to England. But Jerry was adamant about taking me across the big pond with him and, to muck up matters even more, announcing to the world that we were wed, which he wanted to do on-air with Dick Clark before we left for the tour. Jerry felt certain that as king of rock-and-roll the public loved him so much they wouldn't care about his young second-cousin bride.

Can you say "ego?"

Anyway, Jud was saying that Jerry couldn't mess up his upcoming tour of England, which was huge in terms of establishing his career. Jerry thought he was already on top, so wasn't worried about it.

Jud ended up talking on the phone with Clark and his people, and the decision was made that Jerry would not be on the show. He was just too much of a loose cannon and Dick didn't need the grief of promoting someone who could be seen as a cradle-robber.

The flight over the Atlantic Ocean was okay until an engine fire forced us to land in Ireland. We changed planes and finally arrived in London.

One step off the plane and we were assaulted by camera flashes, screams, and people reaching out to touch "the Killer" himself. Oscar escorted Jerry to a spot to be interviewed by the press. The rest of us were left waiting.

That's when the proverbial shit hit the fan. A stray reporter who couldn't get close to Jerry came over and asked me who I was.

"Jerry's wife," I mumbled.

Before I knew it Jerry's agent, Oscar, had me by the arm and was shoving me toward a car.

But it was too late. The cat was out of the bag.

A little while later that reporter showed up at our hotel room door and requested an interview. I let him in. After all, he seemed like a nice enough man. Jerry was there and seemed happy to talk about being married. I chatted away about domestic life. Jerry and I teased each other. We were having fun. Until Oscar arrived. That reporter was booted out and Jerry was taken downstairs to the lobby where an official press conference had been arranged.

Later I heard about how reporters at the press conference went wild asking questions about me. I'd been left alone in our room to stay out of trouble. But when there was a knock at the door, naturally, I answered it, only to find another reporter who wanted to ask me some more questions. I let him in, too. Repeating what Jerry had said to the first reporter, I told him I was fifteen when he asked my age.

Jerry and I thought ourselves clever for our fib about my age. But, wouldn't you know, there would be a reporter who would call overseas to the courthouse in Memphis. Before hanging up on what was a very expensive phone call in those days, he'd discovered that not only was I thirteen years old rather than fifteen when we married, I was Jerry's second cousin. He even found out that Jerry hadn't divorced before marrying me.

I don't know who on earth he talked to in that Memphis courthouse, but I'm betting it was some gossip who to her dying day gloated about revealing the story that brought down the king of rock-and-roll.

The next day the London papers were splattered with my name and picture. In fact, picture after picture. It seemed that every move I'd made outside my room had been photographed. Oscar was beside himself. He said I got more print space than French General de Gaulle's famous retaking of his homeland from the Germans at the end of World War II. Jerry and I had no idea who that was or why Germans had been in France. We had heard of World War II, of course.

Today I look back and see that I was totally unprepared in every way for what took place in England. I didn't know much about different countries or traveling or laws in different places. Or about the unwritten laws of behavior in different cultures. I was so naïve, thinking that everyone thought and lived like I did. I thought that if you were nice to people they would be nice back, and that's all there was to it. How could I have known anything different? I hadn't even stayed in school long enough to be given world history or social studies lessons. So I really wasn't prepared for what happened next.

Crowds of people gathered outside our hotel on Sunday morning after Jerry's first concert the night before. Everybody in the Lewis entourage was relieved to learn that the front desk had called Bobbies, police, to disperse the gaggle of bystanders. Instead, the Bobbies came straight to our room and asked questions about our marriage. Eventually they left to file a report with the Home Office, whatever that was. More newspaper articles informed us that the Ministry of Labor and a number of child welfare organizations were having their say, too. As more and more newspapers demanded that we be deported, with one calling me a "girl victim" of Jerry's bigamy, even a Member of Parliament jumped into the fray, declaring us to be a bad influence on the country's youth.

And all I had ever wanted to do was have a nice little family of my own. I'd certainly never intended to influence anybody about anything.

My sudden notoriety was shocking, appalling, terrifying.

Jerry's shows turned into a disaster. Every show had been sold out but seats were only half filled. He was heckled terribly and his performances, I was told, were lackluster.

In the end, the rest of the tour was canceled as hordes of angry people flooded the street outside our London hotel room. Bobbies fought them off while we fled out a side door to a waiting limousine. Our guise didn't work, though, and the rabid crowd surrounded the car, shaking it until we thought it would turn over. Rusty was crying; I was crying; my mother thought we were going to die.

Finally the driver got away and sped off to the airport. There we consoled ourselves that when we got home we'd be welcomed with open arms by fans who understood and loved us.

How is it possible for one young couple to be so wrong so many times?

Back home Jerry went from making $10,000 a concert to making $250 a night in a dive. For years the press blamed his marriage to me for destroying his career. But, as you know, Jerry's talent rose out of the dust and prevailed. After about ten years, he was back on top. He's still playing concerts, including huge events in England, where his notoriety and fame have done nothing but swell with faithful fans over the years.

I, on the other hand, only went back to England once years later, to promote my book *Great Balls of Fire*. People were gracious, but the memory of that terrifying first visit there still haunts me. I look forward to a time when I can go back to England and visit with Jerry's fan, a time when we can talk and "laugh" about the first visit.

13. **California Dreamin'** | 1958

After the fallout in England, my Daddy decided he needed to broaden his horizons in the music industry. Because of the scandal over my marriage to Jerry Lee, his band had lost its ability to make top dollar. J.W. Brown started looking for other ways to make some money in music.

He had another younger cousin, Mickey Gilley, who was also enormously talented. Maybe he wasn't the showman or showoff that Jerry was, but he was gifted all the same.

By then Mickey had moved to Houston, Texas, and was established there. He had a country-western band and was a good songwriter as well as piano player and singer. Daddy knew our family would never want to move away to Texas and that he wouldn't be part of this cousin's band, but he wanted to see if he could help Mickey take his career into the big time.

He felt certain Mickey had what it took and it turned out he was right.

Daddy had connections in Los Angeles, agents and other music business people, so Mickey, my mom, and he went out there to see what they could drum up.

At that time I was living with the Lewis family, awaiting the birth of our first child. When the money stopped coming in Jerry and I sold our sweet little house on Dianne Lane. He was still touring but had gone from making big bucks to barely scraping by. He was on the road a lot, trying to get that great ball of fire cracklin' again.

So while my parents were in California it was important

to me to talk to them on the phone. I was lonely and missed them terribly. But in those days a long distance call was $15 or more, so we didn't talk often. We did talk enough for me to keep up with what was going on in far-away Hollywood-land.

Unfortunately, while they were there my daddy caught a terrible case of the mumps, of all things. He became terribly sick and could hardly leave the motel room. He wasn't nearly as much help to Mickey as he'd hoped to be. But, as you probably know, Mickey did okay in spite of that.

Even though Daddy got sick, they did meet with some moguls who gave my momma as much attention as they gave the men. Maybe even more. I've always believed that my mom could easily have been a celebrity in her own right. At age twenty-nine, Lois Brown was a beautiful woman in the prime of her life. She had dark brown eyes, an olive complexion, jet black hair, and a figure that reminded people of Marilyn Monroe. When she opened her mouth to speak, her Southern drawl was like sweet honey dripping all over the place. The booking agents offered her a contract on the spot, to work in movies. They would create an image for her as a female "Andy Griffin." Andy had a joke record out called "What it was, was football," which was a big hit. They wanted a female version of that for her.

Her response was, "Gentlemen, I thank you but I have a five-year-old son at home. Actually, I have two children at home, including that big one over there," she said, pointing to her husband. She had no interest in the possibility of being a movie star.

Another fun story about my mom in California is that once they were stopped at a red light and a man in the car beside them hollered at her that she should be in movies. Even strangers saw it. But she didn't want to do that. She liked her family life just as it was.

I, too, hoped for a nice family life of my own. But fear crept into my mind as I awaited the birth of my first child while living with Jerry's parents. This marriage thing wasn't as easy as I'd pictured it would be. I had no idea what was yet to come.

14. **Living with the Lewis Clan** | 1959

When I was six months pregnant with our first child, Jerry sent me to live with his family while he toured. He had two sisters, Frankie Jean and Linda Gail, still living at home with their mom and dad, Mamie and Elmo. Jerry was the oldest living child. The first son had been Elmo, Jr., who was killed in an accident when he was nine years old. Jerry had been a baby at the time. Then came Frankie Jean, and Linda Gail was the youngest.

We were all living at a farm in Clayton, Louisiana, six miles from Ferriday. Clayton was nothing but a wide spot in the road. It had a post office, a grocery store operated by the mayor, a school, a caution light, and one place to eat, a drive-in called the "Toot and Tell." I never ate there; I couldn't stop laughing long enough to go inside.

The house in Clayton had two bedrooms, two closets in one bedroom, no closet in the other bedroom, one bath, a big eat-in kitchen and a giant-sized living room. The front porch had been enclosed as a part of the living room and it had more square footage than the rest of the house. The furniture was placed against the walls and I can remember yelling across the room, trying to carry on a conversation. Then there was this huge area in the center of the room with nothing. There were two or three sofas that made into beds and one spinet piano for Jerry to play when he wasn't on tour. There were thirty-five acres that Jerry's daddy farmed.

This was now the family home, a place Jerry bought for

his family with one of his royalty checks, when he was still getting big royalty checks. And it was the place he sent me to live when I was pregnant because he wanted this child delivered (in a makeshift hospital where roaches ran up the walls) by the same doctor that had saved Jerry's life when he was six months old, Dr. Ratcliff. I, of course, had no voice in this decision.

Late at night I would get out of bed and stare into the pitch darkness, mentally counting how many days I had left to live. I was certain I would die giving birth and fear kept me from asking. I didn't pick out a name for my baby because I never expected to see it. My days were getting fewer and fewer. In my heart I was positive I was going to die. I was horrified and sad, but silent.

I dared not ask anyone for fear that they would confirm my fears. On one of my first visits with my new doctor he asked if I was nauseated and I shook my head indicating no. But before I left I asked if he could give me something to help me stop vomiting.

I missed my parents' house and wanted to go home to them. I wanted to go to my own doctor, but I knew that would not happen. Jerry wasn't about to let any man other than Dr. Ratcliff put his hands on me.

Early in the morning of February 2nd, 1959, Buddy Holly, Ritchie Valence and The Big Bopper's plane crashed in an Iowa cornfield during a snowstorm, killing all on board. The newspapers called it "the day the music died." Now I had one more thing to fear. What would I do if Jerry had been on that tour and on that plane? I had turned fifteen in July. What would I do if something happened to him? I had no answers. I just had one more thing to worry about.

My parents were in California with Mickey Gilley and I missed them. The timing was so bad.

I was alone, afraid, and sad that I would never see my family again. Daddy and Momma sat in a hotel room for almost two weeks in California while Daddy had the mumps. At the same time, I sat and waited to die in Louisiana. My baby was due March 5th or 6th. Even when I did talk to them I never shared my fears. I knew it would worry my mother to death. They had enough to deal with without my problems.

I have always maintained that I was very mature when Jerry and I were married. In retrospect, I can see clearly now that I was older than my years. I considered others first, even to a fault. My desires never came first; instead I always considered the other person. How would they feel? Would it hurt them? If so, I remained silent. It wasn't shyness; it wasn't ignorance; it was concern.

Once while living in Clayton I was driving to Ferriday and came upon a wreck. An elderly man had run into a tractor and was lying on the pavement unconscious. I was the first on the scene and immediately jumped from my car, went over to him, knelt down, and started earnestly praying for this man not to die. Soon an ambulance came, and loaded the injured man and me along with him. I rode the two to three miles to the hospital with him. I had been spotted in the ambulance and it was all over town that someone in the Lewis family had been taken to the hospital. The Lewis' knew about it before the man and I arrived at the hospital! The entire family was there five minutes after we arrived. I was shocked to see them and couldn't figure out how they knew. There's nothing like "life in a small town."

Weeks later someone called investigating the accident asking if I had seen it happen. I told them "no," that I had just "come upon it." They thought I was a family member. I told them I didn't know who he was. Then they said, "But didn't you ride in the ambulance with him?" I said, "Yes, but I still don't know who he is." I took a lot of kidding for a long time about that. I never regretted what I did, and wonder if God may have answered my prayers and let the man live. Who knows for sure?

One thing I can say about the Lewis family is that they knew how to laugh. Their house was often a roar of laughter, laughing at themselves and telling stupid things they had done.

I will always remember how Linda Gail and I were left alone late one December afternoon at the farm in Clayton. The Christmas tree was heavily decorated, presents were stacked high. She and I laughed and joked about unwrapping our gifts for a quick peek at our Christmas presents. Two beautifully wrapped boxes had caught our eye. We both had identically wrapped boxes with the same wrapping paper and huge bows. We often shook them, but they just rustled a little. That certain day we did more than shake the box. Carefully we unstuck the tape, so as not to tear it, slipped the shiny paper off, and out slid the most beautiful white satin robes we'd ever seen. We put our gifts on and wore them around the house acting silly, swishing our long robes, acting like Loretta Young making a grand entrance. They were so decadent and luxurious we hated to put them back in the boxes, and while we were at it we peeked at all of our presents, like a couple of kids left alone.

Christmas morning we were not very happy, it was

such a letdown. The thrill of Christmas morning was gone. Everyone had surprise gifts except Linda and me. We knew what was in every box that had our name on it. You'd think we were children, but in looking back I realize we were. We looked at each other as if to say, we'll never do that again. I was the oldest at fifteen and Linda was only twelve, and we learned our lesson that day. No more peeking. But we never confessed. At least I didn't 'til now.

Linda, though younger than me, was my size. We wore the same size 6 shoe, same size gloves, same bathing suit size and so on, but I was 5' 1" tall and Linda 5'9". She was all legs....

A few weeks after Christmas Linda came waltzing into that huge living room wearing her beautiful white robe but now it stopped above her knee, the sleeves didn't make it to her elbows, and the body of it had gotten so tight she looked like she was wearing a child's clothes and that she'd had a gigantic spurt of growth. It was hilarious. When I stop laughing, I asked her, "What happened?" It seems someone threw her beautiful satin robe in the washer, then the dryer. We suspected Frankie did it. From that day on I guarded my robe, hanging it out of sight for fear it would meet the same fate.

My first child was a boy. Despite all of my fears I survived his birth just fine. We named him Steve after Steve Allen, who had given Jerry his first chance on The Steve Allen Show on TV in 1957. We called our baby Stevie. Even though I was such a young mother, I loved our son beyond measure. My adolescent hope was that our lives were finally going to settle down and we'd be a normal family.

Ah, the innocence of youth.

15. **Too Much Too Soon** | 1959

Jerry's sister Frankie Jean had a reputation—that she lived up to—that she was not to be messed with, ever since the day her older brother, Jerry, came home to change into his new shirt to go out on the town, and words were spoken between Jerry and Frankie. Although no one remembers exactly what was said, an argument ensued and Frankie ripped Jerry's brand new shirt off his back and left a few scratches along the way for good measure.

"Poor Frankie" was what she was referred to by most of the family when she was not in hearing distance. So far life had not been kindhearted to Frankie. She'd married for the first time at age twelve—I'm not kidding, and you thought I was young—and she married for the second time at age fifteen. Then she promptly gave birth to three babies in thirty months. Never thereafter did she have a moment of peace. She was organized and precise yet had not one spare moment to herself.

Then I remember the horrible night her youngest baby, three-month-old Michael Lee, died. Frankie Jean and I had gone to wash and fold diapers at the wash-a-teria. All three of her babies were in diapers, and seeing that these were the days of real cloth diapers that had to be laundered, you can just imagine how much we always had to do. My baby hadn't been born yet, so I was helping her with hers.

Upon our return from the wash-a-teria Frankie checked

on her sleeping babies, but her youngest, Michael Lee, was gone. She rushed back to ask her daddy, Elmo, where the child was. Her dad jumped up and said, "I just put him down. He was asleep."

Within minutes they retrieved the unconscious baby from between the wall and bed. They said it was "crib death."

As if that wasn't bad enough, having a wandering, evil-eyed husband tipped the scales for Frankie Jean.

One night she found her wayward husband out at a time and place when he was supposed to be at work. She never bothered to get out of her mother's Oldsmobile. She just pointed her pistol and shot straight through the windshield. Luckily for him, she missed, but he had a slight limp for a few days thereafter. I'm sure he had never run so fast in his life and likely pulled a muscle. No one even asked about the bullet hole in the windshield. No one dared.

It was all too much, too soon for Frankie Jean. It would have been for most of us.

16. Evening in Paris | 1959

In all of our years together, the only present Jerry himself actually bought for me with his own hands was in 1959. He just wasn't a present-buying kind of guy. Of all the places in the world he traveled, this gift was bought at an American service station.

In the slow pace of the '50s, you'd drive into a service station, and a man in greasy clothes would greet you and ask, "How much gas ya want? Fill 'er up?"

You'd reply, "Fill 'er up with high test."

They pumped your gas, wiped your windshield, and checked your oil, all as you sat in the car watching them do it. That's just how it was back then. Gasoline was thirty cents a gallon.

Later Jerry told me of how he and the band, en route home from a three-weeklong tour, stopped to gas up the car. Back then, lots of groups on tour drove around the country. People just didn't fly around in planes like they do today. So they were filling up and as it turned out this station had gifts inside by the Coke machine, stacked on the counter with hand-written price tags. Not something you usually saw in a 1950's gas station. Included among the gifts was a beautiful, royal blue, satin, heart-shaped box that contained four lovely bottles of the same intoxicating fragrance—Evening in Paris—and it was beautiful!

It caught me by surprise. It tickled me, imagining him meandering to the Coke machine, dropping in a nickel for a six ounce cold Coca-Cola, which all good Southern boys drank, and spotting the gift-wrapped boxes. He probably thought, "Well, after all, it is December and Christmas is around the corner. Myra will like this. Yes, she will."

It was a heartwarming act, not something Jerry was known for. He was usually content at Christmastime to hand me a fistful of hundred dollar bills and tell me to go buy "whatever" I wanted from him. It could be a new Cadillac or a new pair of shoes; the cost didn't matter. But we both always knew it wasn't really from him. However, this royal blue box with a satin bow and four small bottles inside had his fingerprints all over it, making it far more meaningful than any present under any of my Christmas trees. The lift it gave my spirit just to know that he thought of me without any prompting made tears well up in my eyes.

Long after the fragrances had dissipated I kept the box tucked away, wrapped tightly in paper, until years later when I had to toss it away because of the memories it aroused in my heart. When you can't look at something without crying, it needs to go. That is, if you are ever to move on with your life. When you hold tight to painful memories, some part of your heart has not accepted the reality. Letting go hurts really badly for the time being but holding on hurts every day forever.

Even now a whiff of Evening in Paris would surely bring tears to my eyes. There are some things the heart never forgets and just maybe...the heart has a mind of its own.

17. **A Test of Life: Stevie's Death** | 1962

Losing a child. Unless you've been through it, there is no way to understand the pain of this heartbreak. It's every parent's worst nightmare. Nothing on earth comes close to this gut wrenching, heartbreaking horror.

Children are supposed to bury their parents, not the other way around. A life of three years is hardly a lifetime. That's how long our Stevie lived.

Life as I knew it came to an end Easter Sunday, April 22, 1962, when my world fell apart. You beg God to stop your heart from beating, to please just let you die. There is nothing to compare with this agony and loss.

It's a pain that never goes away.

Friends take all medication, guns, and knifes from your home, knowing you would do anything to stop this hurt. Knowing you want to be with your child so he won't be alone.

Your mind tries to convince you it's all a bad dream, then you awake and reality sets in.

This is the most pain a parent will ever endure; this knife stays in your heart, twisting and turning to inflict inexplicable pain.

I was sleeping and having a horrible nightmare that my son had drowned. I awoke with a jolt telling myself, "It must be a nightmare. It must be a nightmare!" I crawled from my bed and don't recall how I thought I traveled from my home to Jerry's mother's house, but I opened the door and there straight ahead in her living room sat a tiny baby casket by the window. I remember screaming and falling to the floor. Jerry picked me up in his arms and put me back in our own bed as I sobbed and screamed from the vision I'd had in my sleep. "Please, God," I wailed, "let me die. I cannot stand this pain."

In the light of day a morsel of sanity would return and I would know the truth. Our child had died in a stupid, freak accident. They always say that children can disappear in a second.

I know this to be true.

Stevie had been sitting down on the walkway in the front yard playing with a toy while Jerry's dad Mr. Lewis, Elmo, and I stood there talking. I was telling him what I needed from the store to make dinner. He and Jerry's Uncle George, who was also there in the yard with us, were staying for dinner. They'd driven from Louisiana to bring Stevie home to me. I'd been out of town for four or five days with Jerry on tour and our boy had spent that time with his grandparents. But I came home to spend Easter with Stevie. We'd gone to church that morning and I was happy to have my little one back in my arms.

As I rattled off the groceries I needed, Elmo said, "You need to write that down."

I agreed, "It's too much for anyone who doesn't cook to remember."

As we stepped inside so I could write a list I said, "Uncle George, will you be right here to watch Stevie?"

He nodded "yes."

We went in, I grabbed a piece of paper and wrote down

the items, and I explained one of them to my father-in-law. We walked back outside and I didn't see Stevie.

"George, where's Stevie?" I couldn't keep the panic from my voice.

He said, "He went back in the house right after you."

I went back in and started calling him. When there was no answer I looked in each bedroom, still calling his name. He could sit and play alone with a toy as quiet as a mouse, so I knew that calling alone wouldn't bring him to me. I had to keep looking and find him.

By the time I'd covered the whole house and realized he wasn't there, my heart was pounding. Frantic now, I ran to the pool in the backyard. When I spied a green garden hose trailing into the pool, the hose Stevie had played with earlier in the day in the front yard, I screamed.

In the blink of an eye our neighbor, Bill Haney, who'd been out in his front yard, appeared. Without hesitation he dove into the pool and rose up from the water with something in his arms.

I remember screaming and falling to the ground and fainting.

Then I saw people everywhere. I thought surely I was having a bad, bad dream. This couldn't be real. I would awake any second.

It seemed like a thousand people were there. It became dark out and people just kept coming to my house.

I don't recall much after that. They said I disappeared after the funeral, which I don't remember, and they found me lying on the ground beside my baby's grave.

A piece of my heart is still there.

18. **Babes in Angel Arms** | Mid-'60s

After the loss of Stevie, the family stood in the family cemetery once again to bury a child.

First there had been Michael Lee, Jerry's sister Frankie Jean's youngest, who died of crib death. Then there was Stevie.

There we were again for the burial of little three-year-old Tammy, Jimmy Swaggart's niece. Again, it was one of those unimaginable tragedies, the kind that every parent has nightmares about.

Tammy's papaw (Jimmy's daddy) was going to the store. Tammy's mother, Jeannette (Jimmy's sister), was sick in bed.

Tammy said, "I want to go with Papaw!"

So Jeannette told her to run out and tell him to let her go, which Tammy did.

But her grandfather said, "I can't take you with me today. Now go back inside and I'll come back to see you later today."

With that he drove away.

Instead of going inside, Tammy apparently thought she might just go visiting for a while.

Hours later Papaw returned to visit his grandbaby only to learn that she never came back inside. Jeanette thought Tammy was with Papaw and Papaw thought she'd gone back inside her home. But all the while the little girl was roaming the neighborhood alone.

Later it was discovered that this little girl wandered

around for hours. People said she went into the store where her Papaw was at the same time. But they didn't happen to see each other.

And a neighbor spotted Tammy standing alone looking down at the turbulent swirling water of the creek, over-flowing from an early spring rain that had pounded Baton Rouge for days. The woman stopped and told the three-year-old to go on home… and drove away. The woman was never able to justify why she didn't pick the child up and take her home.

They found Tammy's tiny body the next morning down-stream about a mile from where she was last seen. It was a "perfect storm" for all involved. It was just overwhelming that this small child wondered her neighborhood for hours and no one put the pieces together to realize the danger and get her safely back home.

I think of that every time I see a little one alone any-where—in a store, on a sidewalk, riding a bike in the street—an alarm goes off in my heart and I immediately look for the adult who needs to be close at hand. If there isn't one, I take the child and go find one. It's a kind of warning we should all heed.

19. **Roping Phoebe** | 1963

Phoebe Lewis was the cutest infant girl in the world. As her mother I was, of course, sure of that, as so many mothers are of their own infants.

She was born in 1963, only sixteen months after the loss of our first baby, Stevie. Phoebe was a big surprise to her daddy because in his mind real men have boys. So how did this girl get into the mix? Male chauvinist pig, perhaps?

But that didn't last long. By the time this blue-eyed toddler in her footed pajamas was big enough to crawl onto her daddy's lap he was smitten. She may not have been a boy but she had stolen her daddy's heart. As she got older, heart-shaped gifts and tokens became their symbol that "Phoebe is Daddy's heart." It was a love that transcended all others.

Before she could even walk Phoebe was trying to climb her way out of anything. When she was a year old I found her one night balancing on the side of her crib, about to fall onto our terrazzo (concrete) floor. That could have either killed her or caused brain damage. The crib came down the next day and was replaced by a twin bed. When I expressed concern to her pediatrician about her ability to pull herself out of her crib, he told me she was too little to do that. Of course, I knew better. I bought a twin mattress and put it on the floor beside her bed, for soft landings when she tumbled out at night.

By the time she could walk, it took a couple of adults

who were on their toes to manage her. She had more energy than her body could handle. Thank goodness I had Lottie, my maid, who was so much like family she even named one of her children Myra after me. Lottie had been with me for years and was family as far as we were all concerned. The two of us would sit and watch *Love of Life* on television at 11:00 a.m. every weekday. This was a soap opera that ran for years and years, and we were unmistakably addicted. We stopped whatever we were doing to catch up on this "real life story."

As if we didn't have enough drama in our own lives.

Sometimes Lottie would take Phoebe out to play and I would do the cleaning. Phoebe could wear out two adults before noon any day of the week and twice on Sunday.

Riding with Phoebe in my car was always an adventure. I loved my "caterpillar green" Mercury station wagon. Remember that there were no seatbelts in the '60s, which could create a problem with children who didn't want to go where you were taking them. Driving and trying to hold on to Phoebe at the same time was a real challenge.

At one point she was yelling that she wanted to go to Mom's house (my mother's house). I tried to convince her that we were on our way there but she wouldn't hear of it. She wanted to be there "now."

From the back seat she tried to open the door. She was getting out! I still don't know how I was able to reach her and keep the car in the road at the same time on a four-lane road at fifty miles an hour. But I managed to grab her and drag her into the front seat with me. And I didn't take my one hand off of her until we were at my parents' house.

When we got home I went to the garage and found a

rope. I tied up every door on my car, attaching the rope from the looped door handles to the luggage rack on top, first one door then the next door and the next door, all except the driver's door. From that day on, if you wanted to get into my car, the only entrance was the driver's door.

I would see drivers laughing at me as I drove along with this precious little daughter trying to kick open the door tied with ropes.

We cut the ropes off when I traded in the Mercury a few years later. I miss those ropes. I needed seatbelts and handcuffs to restrain Phoebe. She bounced and jumped and kicked her way through her childhood car rides.

However, I am proud to say she does use her seatbelt now.

20. **What Happened to the Duck?** | 1967

The last place you'd ever want to be was in a car on a "way too long trip" with Phoebe. It was always an experience to remember for a long time.

We were taking a trip to visit Jerry's family in Louisiana. We decided my station wagon would be the best car to take since I had a small mattress in the back where Phoebe could work off some of her wild energy by bouncing around. I brought books to read to her, too, and that would settle her down somewhat for a short while.

This particular trip Jerry was driving, which was unusual for him as he was accustomed to being driven around. But I was in the backseat with Phoebe, reading to her.

It was a story about a little lost baby duck looking for its mother. The little duck had gone everywhere asking everyone if they had seen her mother. It made one wonder if she was ever going to be reunited with her mother or would she be a lost orphan duck alone in the world forever. She would go up to a machine and ask, "Are you my Mother?" The baby duck was really lost!

Fear mounted that the baby may never see her mother again....

I stopped for a moment to take a drink of my cold Coca-Cola, and suddenly from the driver's seat I heard a shout. "What happened to the duck?"

It seems that Phoebe's daddy was also enjoying this children's story. When I stopped reading at a critical moment the tension in the driver's seat exploded. It was amusing to see this grown man demanding to know what happened to the duck.

I continued to read to Phoebe for years and I always considered there just might be someone else listening so I didn't stop until the dramatic ending.

21. **Weren't They Just Precious?** | 1967

The problem was half of the parenting Phoebe received. Jerry's belief was, "If you love your child, you will let them do whatever they want to do." Jerry was raised by his mother with no rules and was never told "no." I know, that's explains a lot. Anyway, Jerry and I had many disagreements about this. I felt a child needed discipline and needed to be taught how to behave in public. They needed to know they were not going to get everything they wanted because that is not how life really is. They will ruin their own life and never find happiness unless they know how to share, how to give and take. They need to know how to treat others kindly. They need to learn to discipline themselves. Life is too complex to think you can have your way all the time.

I understood that my work was cut out for me; and that getting these lessons across to my beloved but devilish daughter was going to be no easy task.

However, due to Jerry's philosophy of permissiveness, there were some outstanding moments I'll never forget.

I remember this one like it was yesterday. Phoebe was about four years old and insisted on standing in front of the television with her arms outstretched so no one could see it.

In his sweetest voice Jerry said, "Move, darlin'."

"No!" was the response.

In a nice sing-song voice Jerry said, "Now move, baby. Daddy's watching TV."

"No!"

THE SPARK THAT SURVIVED

By now, Jerry had reached the end of his being-nice rope. He yelled, "Move dammit!"

At this point his precious daughter drew back her sweet little arm and threw the sharp pencil she'd been holding in her precious little hand. It struck her wonderful father smack dab in the middle of the forehead.

He jumped up and chased after her while she ran as fast as her fat little legs could go. He didn't even come close to catching her as she zigzagged down the hall and into a bedroom to shimmy under a bed. Daddy couldn't reach her and she wasn't about to come out.

Weren't they both just precious?

I thought this no discipline thing just may work—at least to entertain me.

I laughed my ass off all over again writing about it today.

22. **Priscilla and Me** | 1960s

At the same time that Jerry and I were married and living in Memphis, Tennessee, Priscilla Wagner was living there with her longtime boyfriend Elvis Presley. They eventually married in 1967, but had dated from the time she was fourteen. Priscilla and I were about the same age, we both lived with rock-and-roll stars, and we were in the same town, so you'd think we would have become friends. I used to fantasize I could get to know her because she seemed like a nice person. I imagined that she was one of the few people on earth who would understand what my life was like because she also lived with the endless touring and celebrity. Maybe we could comfort each other.

But with the animosity that Jerry felt toward Elvis, whose career had continued to soar because, unlike Jerry, he had not married his underage girlfriend, a friendship between us two women could never have happened.

I used to think of Priscilla when I'd wake up looking at the electrical socket on the wall by the baseboard. That was my view upon waking because I often slept on the twin mattress on the floor, the one that had been put in our bedroom under Phoebe's crib when she was a toddler in case she crawled out and tumbled to the floor. It's interesting to me today that even though my sleeping on the floor didn't seem right to me, back then I didn't have the maturity or strength to question it.

That was where I slept when Jerry came home from tour. Usually he was on tour for all but about ten days every three months. The minute he came home his mother, father, younger sister, some of the band members, other people who worked for him, and a friend or two would descend upon our house. So I cooked and waited on the houseful of people until he left for his next tour. The moment he left, so did all of our guests.

When they were there they filled all of the bedrooms, including Phoebe's room. That left her coming back into our bedroom with Jerry and me. Because I didn't want my child to sleep on the floor, I'd put her in the bed and bunk down on the mattress myself. It had never been taken out of the room because we needed it during these invasions.

Sleeping on the floor didn't really bother me all that much. Yet I'd open my eyes, look at the socket, and wonder if Priscilla slept on the floor at Elvis' house. Of course, I knew she did not. And I knew that I shouldn't have to do that, either. I just didn't know what to do—yet—about it.

I didn't know what Priscilla Presley's life was like in the privacy of their home, but I suspected it was nothing like mine. I did know that Elvis wanted the exact opposite out of his wife's appearance than Jerry wanted out of me. She was always made up to perfection and looked the part of a star's glamorous wife. I, on the other hand, had to look like a well-scrubbed church-going woman. My husband wouldn't let me cut my hair because in his twisted mind it was a sin for a woman to cut her hair.

I couldn't even begin to understand that one.

My church lady appearance didn't suit my personality and I always resented that Jerry never warned me about his beliefs before we were married. I hadn't known I'd have to remake myself and that my own personality would be stripped away, along with my confidence and self-esteem. (Maybe that explains me today: always wearing make-up and trying to get my hair to look just so!)

All of this was so that no other man would care to look at me. It wasn't right; it wasn't fair; and I wish I had had the guts and gumption to refuse to go along with this. But, of course, once my confidence had been squashed I didn't have the nerve to stand up to him.

The truth is I didn't want to meet Priscilla. In spite of my daydream that we had some things in common, I was far too insecure to want to actually meet her. I avoided her at all costs.

We both went to the same hair salon across the street from Graceland. Jerry would let me go for a wash and curl, so the salon was one of my regular outings, which I enjoyed. They talked about Priscilla in the salon so I knew she was a regular, too, but I hadn't ever run into her there. Then one day I saw her coming and I actually went out the backdoor. I was far too intimidated to take a chance on meeting her. I didn't know what to do.

What would I say? "Hello, Priscilla. I've been wondering: Do you ever sleep on a mattress on the floor at Graceland?"

All that meeting Priscilla Presley would do, I imagined, was highlight my own personal shortcomings and strange home life in comparison.

It took years for me to grow up enough to realize that a wife should not be treated the way I was being treated. A wife should be treated the way my daddy treated my momma. I finally realized that I deserved the same thing. If I wasn't going to get it in this marriage, I would have to move on to get it.

When that realization came, I had to make the agonizing choice that so many women make, to leave my husband and start a new life. Priscilla, as it turned out, did the same thing.

In the end, we both had our crosses to bear. We had more in common than I ever imagined.

23. **Welcome to Howard Johnson's** | 1960s

I once counted the actual amount of time that J.L.L. and I spent alone in our home at night out of thirteen years of marriage. It was only two weeks; fourteen days all total. All I needed was a big orange garbage can out front and I could have been a Howard Johnson Motel.

I always thought it was so awful of all of those people—Jerry's family, band members, and hangers-on—to make me share Jerry with all of them. I seldom had any time with him alone. I suspected that some of them relished the idea that was the way it was going to stay.

That was especially true when Jerry never failed to let me know beyond a doubt that his mother came first in his life, over anyone. I wondered how he would take it if I had announced that my daddy was my number one person in the world. I shudder just imagining…! But in his mind he was privileged and I, simply, was not.

I fully understood that they were always poor and that Jerry, once he became famous and made big money, was their way out of poverty. I accepted that but you would have thought I had contrived to get Jerry to marry me and planned on cutting them off from the money.

They hated me on sight. I was too young to know that for the longest time.

However, my father-in-law, Jerry's daddy Elmo Lewis,

was not a part of the "hate team." Bless his heart; he was a gentle soul and a good man. He was also my great uncle, of course.

In fact, I'd taken to calling Jerry's parents Mr. and Mrs. Lewis rather than their first names. Before marrying Jerry I'd always known them as Aunt Mamie and Uncle Elmo. After our marriage Jerry pointed out that if I continued to call them aunt and uncle it only emphasized the fact that he and I were cousins. So, being a kid after all, I took to calling them by more formal names.

Odd, to say the least.

24. The Cheating Chapter | 1970

Not that I felt I was anyone special, but I was a faithful wife to Jerry. I would have fought a circus off for him. I praised him to the highest and defended him to the bitter end. I was completely convinced that J.L.L. was everything good I thought he was and that we were going to grow old together. Our love for each other would never fade. Plain and simple, I loved the man. He loved me.

There was nothing I had done or failed to do that brought this horrible fate down upon me. What is it about some men that they believe they are above rules? *Do as I say, not as I do.*

Somewhere around 1968 Jerry started changing. He would call me after his show was over as late as 2:00 or 3:00 a.m. He was argumentative and accused me of every sin on God's green earth. He would scream profanities at me and curse me until he ran out of words; then he'd start over and repeat himself. It was as if a demon had possessed him.

Finally, I would break down sobbing and beg him to tell me "why" he was so angry at me. He never answered the question.

The next afternoon he'd call me laughing and kidding, as if nothing had happened. He was his old self. When I asked why he was talking to me like that the night before, he just laughed and swore he didn't mean a word of it, that he was just tired and needed sleep. I would tell him how much I loved him and I would beg him not to ever do that again.

I told him I missed him and swore my deepest devotion to him, that I loved him more than he would ever know and that I was a good wife...and that he shouldn't talk to me that way.

Then the very next night the devil/prince-of-darkness would call again and a demon's voice would say to me, "Who the hell do you think you are?" I'd ask him please not to call me like this in the middle of the night and he'd say he could call whenever he wanted to. I was caught in this vicious cycle. The next morning a different "husband" called in and we went through the same conversation as the day before.

This went on for several years with me hoping and praying that the very next conversation with Jerry would convince him to change back to the Jerry I knew, the Jerry I had married. Now I know that this is very common for abused women. Hope—unwarranted though it might be—keeps us in the relationship, even when the same abuse happens time and again. Remember the movie *Groundhog Day*? I lived it, over and over and over.

I was unaware that Jerry had started taking drugs. Someone—a fan, a friend, a monster—had introduced him to some seriously bad drugs that turned him into Lucifer himself. This was not the man I married. The playful silliness we had together was gone. My life revolved around a 3 a.m. phone call where I was told how ugly I was, how stupid I was, and that I had better "straighten up" because no man would ever have me if he left me. My life was a living hell. I didn't know what to do except to plead my case to him on those nightly calls. I attempted not answering the phone. That failed miserably. Jerry called my parents, who lived a few blocks away, at 2 a.m. and told them to "go tell Myra to put the phone on the hook." I didn't try that again. I wouldn't do that to my parents. Like so many abused women, I was ashamed and didn't want my family to know how bad it was.

My health started to fail, my nerves were crumbling. I dreaded seeing him leave on tour because this monster-demon would be calling me again. I remember one bad night in particular after the dreaded phone call. I went into my back yard. Even though it was a cold and damp October night, I threw myself on the ground as I clawed at the dirt. I prayed, "God, please let me die." The cold wet grass didn't bother me but the pain in my heart did; it wouldn't go away. I didn't know what more I could do to change this. I had begged and pleaded and cried with no results. It was then that something happened that I describe in the next chapter, something that was bigger than me. I was at the end of my rope, but that rope somehow grew longer.

I had discovered that everything I had ever believed about my marriage was a lie.

My husband's betrayal. How could I have been so blind?

Jerry always said, "Marry 'em young and bring 'em up the way you want them to be." I didn't know that also included, "…and the way you want them to believe."

He broke my heart, broke my spirit, and broke my will to live.

The night I was told the truth came right out of the blue with a phone call from a stranger. This voice I'd never heard before in my life told me that my husband had sex with women all over the country while he was on tour.

My whole world shattered in that instant. I couldn't pretend any longer. I couldn't continue to live in my childish hopes and dreams. This wasn't a Disney fairytale or Hollywood movie. This was real life. My life. And it wasn't going to have a happy ending.

As dedicated as I had always been to my husband, I didn't doubt what the unknown woman said. Pieces to the puzzle of Jerry's bizarre behavior fell into place. The drugs. The accusations. The mistrust. He'd been transferring his own behavior onto me.

I didn't know what to do, so I drove to my church, Barton Heights Church of God. It was late at night but I knew the church doors would be unlocked. They were always unlocked just in case some distressed soul felt the need to bury their face in the altar and cry their heartbreak away. It was the perfect place for me that night.

This was my church, the one I had attended with my three-year-old son Stevie on our last Easter, the Sunday he died. Before the sun had set on that most religious day of the year, my baby was gone from this world. This church was the only place since that had eventually been able to bring me some solace, but on the night that I learned about my husband's betrayal there was nothing that could deliver me from this new agony. I sobbed, unable to speak a word.

My pastor's wife, Sister Davis, knelt beside me and began to pray for me. My sobs were so gut wrenching that I was never able to say one word that she could understand. But she was persistent and just kept asking God to please help me. My cries never stopped.

I had just learned that my husband of thirteen years had committed adultery more times during our marriage than could be counted. I had thought we shared the same values, we loved each other, and there was a bond that would never be broken.

The crazy part is that my husband made me believe that we were cleaved together forever by his preaching to me about sin, the worst of all being adultery. He ranted and raved about how sinful it would be to be unfaithful. Silly me, I thought he meant both of us when he just meant it for me.

Stupid, damn, double standards. Big difference: A woman couldn't do that unless she was a slut but to a man it was acceptable, not even considered a sin or wrong.

Who was this man I had given the last thirteen years of my life to? Who was this person who had my undying devotion and respect? He was a traitor. He preached one thing and did another. I knew I would never get over this betrayal nor would I ever forgive what he did. A dagger through the heart would have been kinder than this.

Maybe, just maybe, if he had not been so demanding of me, so jealous and overbearing, I would have felt differently. But he had always demanded that I not even look a man in the eye. I had to look at the floor.

Once when I was on a flight by myself I thought the man next to me was trying to flirt. He kept talking to me. Of course, having been trained not to meet eyes with a man, I wouldn't look at him. Finally he said, "Myra, don't you know me? We just met at that charity event with Jerry. I'm Kenny Rogers." I dared glance his way and he didn't look familiar because I hadn't looked at him when we were introduced at the event. He wasn't flirting at all. He was just being kind.

I met a number of famous people; Kris Kristofferson, Johnny Cash, Brenda Lee; and didn't hold conversations with any of them. I'm sure people thought of me as stupid and self-conscious, which I was neither. Or maybe I was stupid. After all, I had believed a lie for half of my life. I was twenty-six years old and had been married thirteen of those years to a damn stranger.

The night that I got that fateful phone call and kneeled in prayer at my church, once again I pleaded, "Dear God, please let me die so this pain will go away."

But God knew my heart and said, "No. I won't let you die, but I will be with you."

Morning came and I finally left the church knowing that I must live, but having little heart for it. I knew I had to go on, however, for my daughter.

For the next five days I never ate a bite of food or drank a sip of water. I was in shock. This was the most difficult time of my life next to losing my son. I was losing everything I had ever believed in. Jerry, I thought, was my soul mate, but now I knew him to be a stranger who had lied to me and abused me. I did not know him! Our life together had been one big lie.

Jerry's explanation was "they meant nothing." Well, they should have meant something for the price that was paid by both of us. They should have meant a hell of a lot. Those other women might not have meant anything to him, but they meant everything to me.

Years later he confessed to me that he started sleeping around just eleven months into our marriage.

Was this all happening because I was so young and naive or was it because I was dumb? For a while I blamed myself, until I realized I had done nothing to make this happen. Those were his choices, not mine. I would pay a dear price alright, but not due to my choices. It was the price for my refusal to go on living as if nothing had happened and nothing was wrong.

It was wrong. And I would not live with that.

25. **The Walk-In** | 1970

I died that night in my backyard.

Splayed out on the ground, clawing at the dirt I wished could be my grave, the naïve girl with fairytale dreams left my body.

Another being took her place.

I don't know if it was divine intervention by God, the guidance of a guardian angel, the strong spirit of my great-grandmother Arilla, some unknown entity, or the rekindling of a tiny spark that had survived the great balls of fire. I do know that this body was suddenly empty and just as suddenly inhabited by someone new. I felt it as clearly as I feel my skin.

It was a woman I did not know.

I'm not claiming that woman knew exactly what she was doing—more drama was to come—but I am saying that in the beat of a heart I became a totally different person.

It was as if Myra the girl melted away into that cold, damp earth and a grown woman slipped into the body that was left behind.

I know psychiatrists would probably say I'm nuts, or at the very least it was just a natural maturing of my ability to cope. They would be wrong. This body was now home to a new person.

I suspect there are lots of people who know what I mean. Anybody who has been to that edge of desperation and despair, and somehow got back up to carry on with life, might have that same sense of having died and been reborn.

It was the new me that carried my body into the church to weep the night away. It was the new me that realized I had to live for my daughter. It was the new me who breathed the fresh morning air and knew that life must go on.

Apparently, it just wasn't my time to die.

26. Broken Hearts, Broken Souls, Broken Promises | 1971

Hiring an attorney and filing for divorce in 1971 was excruciating. It was ripping my heart out. My first instinct was to look inward and to question myself harshly, thinking I must have somehow been at fault. What had I done or failed to do... or to be? Over and over again I wondered, "What could I have done differently?" The emotional roller coaster took my breath away. In the quiet of the night I'd torment myself with endless questions.

Finally, I came to accept that I was not the cause of this problem. Jerry was a big boy. He knew right from wrong.

This thing should not have been laid at my doorstep. I was not deserving of the harsh treatment I was inflicting upon myself. In the light of day, I knew I was not to blame. I wasn't the one who had done it and I couldn't have changed it. And I could not live with it.

All of my choices faded from sight, leaving me with no alternative. There was only one answer and my mind knew what it was, but my heart kept fighting me, insisting I hold on to false hope.

I loved Jerry at the same time I hated him for being a hypocrite, for destroying our world with reckless regard. I hated him for demanding I do one thing while he did the exact opposite. I couldn't have loved him any more than I already did, but I could have loved him longer.

I admitted to myself, "This is how the end comes, like a thief in the night."

Jerry and I had been through so much together. We'd buried our first child.

Our second baby, Phoebe, was going on five and she was the love of our life. After losing Stevie my world crashed. I wasn't living; I merely existed. That was until they handed me a pink bundle on August 29, 1963. I looked into those baby blue eyes and knew at that moment why I was alive.

I would watch our child at play and think of all of the complications a divorce would cause. Knowing that she would no longer be with her daddy all the time broke my heart. Those two adored each other.

This was a battle I'd been drafted into against my will, but in it I was. There would be no winners in this war. Everyone would lose.

So there I was, having spent half of my life in a sham of a marriage. I remember sitting on the front porch one night, looking at the bright moon, thinking about how often my husband had told me I was nothing. Suddenly it struck me that if I was nothing that meant I could make myself anything I wanted to be.

Then, like a neon sign from the divorce gods to leave no doubt in my mind, the final nail was hammered into the coffin of that marriage. Seeing that I'd left our home in a rush after finding out about Jerry's infidelities, most of my belongings were still there. I hadn't returned in the short time I'd been gone, even though Jerry had repeatedly called me and begged me to come back to him. He loved me, he said. No one else mattered, he said.

This one afternoon, assuming Jerry would be on the

road or at least out of the house that time of day, I went back to pick up some clothes. Our sweet maid Lottie, who'd become one of my few friends, met me at the door and begged me not to go down the hallway into the bedroom. I appreciated her concern but suddenly knew with no doubt what I had to do. I went down that hall and walked into the bedroom. There was Jerry in bed with a woman I'd never seen before.

Later I was to learn that her name was Jaren. She became his fourth wife, the one who was addicted to drugs and mysteriously drowned in a friend's swimming pool just before her divorce from Jerry was final.

As for my divorce from Jerry, I took my daughter and my broken but mending heart, and moved to Atlanta, Georgia. I was ready to start a new life. Unfortunately, my "start" was rough and I fell into that rebound romance that is so common. I look back and wonder, "What on earth was I thinking?" Duh. Obviously, I wasn't thinking. I suspect I just wanted to show Jerry that I could have someone else, too.

Consequently, a fabulous new life wasn't in the cards for me yet.

27. **The Light in Her Eyes** | 1972

Once Jerry and I divorced, the hardest part was never seeing my daughter's eyes light up at all the toys Santa brought her. I always put her on a plane to her daddy's house for Christmas, and summers, too.

The only way I could get through that was by knowing that Phoebe was happy. All she knew at that point in her life was that both of her parents loved her and that Santa could find her no matter which house she was sleeping in.

I told her to love her daddy, because my problems with him were not her problems. I bent over backwards to instill in her that she was still his baby, that I had a divorce from him but she did not. I have never agreed with husbands and wives who turn their children against each other during a divorce. That's so hurtful to the children.

If you teach a child that their father is bad then they may very well think that since they are his child they, too, are bad. It's a thin line to walk but trying to turn a child against one of the parents is like beating your ex over the head with your child as a weapon. Being an ex-wife is not easy and I was determined that she was not going to be an ex-child.

In the *Bible,* King Solomon tells two women fighting over a baby to cut it in half. But he eventually revealed that a real parent would give up the child to save its life; a real parent would have no part of cutting her child in half. I wouldn't have any part of that, either.

Why should our daughter pay for our problems? Time has proven me right. I did the right thing by my daughter.

I might have missed her excitement at Christmas, but I've been granted a lifetime of love in return. Phoebe Lewis is my best friend. She is the light of my life.

28. **The Next Ship Leaving Port** | 1972

I know I'm not the only woman who's ever fallen into this trap. You will find there's always a more-than-willing man to help you accomplish this, especially when there's a famous name or money involved. You've been told by your ex-husband that no man will ever have you, so pride and revenge take over and before you can say "here comes the bride" you are one.

That's what happened to me. I didn't even like the guy I was going to marry. So why did I? I'm still baffled for a reason, except that he was taking a job in Atlanta, Georgia, and that would get me out of Memphis. I didn't stand a chance of a normal life living in Memphis. All I would ever be was J.L.L.'s ex-wife.

I went through with this wedding but it was really a stupid thing to do. It was a way to slap my ex in the face as well as prove him wrong. So I married this joker and we moved to Atlanta. I put my seven-year-old daughter in school and then I go blank. I can't remember a day-to-day instance during this time at all. This went on for a couple of years. I wasn't happy and I wasn't miserable. I was healing from the blow of the divorce, from the disappointment of Jerry being the kind of man I came to realize he was. I wasn't numb and hurting, but I also wasn't grieving. I was plain and simple "in limbo." A healing process can't start until you go through the grieving stage, which starts with anger and then moves on to a resolve to make a better life for yourself.

I admit I took the coward's way out. Knowing my life would be hell in Memphis, I took a shortcut. That relationship was doomed to fail from day one.

The way it came to an end shocked me. I remember it like it was yesterday. Pete was out of town on business for his company. The phone rang that morning while I was making the bed. It was him saying he was sick and needed a doctor.

I asked what was wrong and he finally got around to saying, "You're my wife and I'm supposed to love you, right?

My answer was, "Yeah, that's how it usually works."

He went on to say, "But I don't care if I ever see you again."

I was surprised but not hurt. So I said to him, "That's not a problem. I can take care of that. I'll see you when you get back."

I hung up the phone and finished making the bed.

I wasn't upset; I wasn't mad....I was relieved.

He showed up in a few days to get his clothes. I watched as he emptied his closet, feeling no emotion whatsoever. I told him my lawyer said this was simple: 30 days was all it took for a non-contested divorce to be done.

He looked a little sheepish, staring down at the floor. Then he asked, "Is it too late to take back what I said?"

I smiled and said, "Oh yes."

I never saw him or spoke to him again. A few months later I found out he'd married a girl and ended up telling her the same thing he told me. His friends believed he was having a hard time accepting the fact that he was gay.

For me life was good. Both closets in the master bedroom were now mine.

29. **Not Without Losing My Mind** | 1974

After my divorces my days were fine. I kept myself busy.

I've always loved to cook and clean so I had an immaculate house. It took me years to realize that when I'm extremely upset I always bake a cake. That would calm me down. Beating the ingredients gave me something physical to "beat." I've been known to walk a yummy, fresh-from-the-oven cake next door and hand it off to a neighbor. It had served its purpose.

Even today I'm known for baking a mean cake. At any moment I can whip one up as I always have the ingredients on hand.

But it's been a long, long time since I baked an "anger cake." Now I bake them just so I can eat them.

Phoebe and I had a lot of quality time together in those days. She never knew back then that she was my rock, my innocent little girl. She'd done nothing to deserve all of this heartache. I knew beyond a shadow of a doubt that getting Phoebe out of a home where Jerry's belief was "never tell a child no" was the right thing to do. I knew I had removed her from a destructive situation. If nothing else I was going to give her a chance at a life that included discipline.

For years after my divorces from Jerry and that other dumbass I married, I would lie awake, night after night, staring at the dark ceiling, going over and over the events of my life. My days were fine, but in the dark of night while I lay in my bed, with no busy-ness to keep me occupied, I'd analyze the past and ask myself the tough questions. Could I have done things

differently? Was I to blame for some of this? Could I have changed any of this?

I cried myself to sleep for about five years.

When the sun came up I crawled from my bed, leaving my doubts and fears safely tucked under my pillow. I'd get up and spill my heartaches onto the pages of my journal, where I hoped they would stay and leave me in peace for this day.

I gave myself marching orders:

"No crying when the sun is up."

"Be strong just for today, just this one day."

"No letting Phoebe know you are sad."

I could do it all day, but when the sun went down so did my strength. This stayed with me even though it didn't affect my ability to function. My past insisted on stalking me in the present, staring me straight in the eye. My heart knew I had I done the right thing. I needed my brain to get on board. I filled my journals, keeping them hidden, which gave me the freedom to express my true feelings. But still, I just couldn't shake it off.

I eventually thought I may benefit by going to counseling. It was the one thing I hadn't done yet.

My very first counseling appointment was a group session. I was curious to see how it would work. About half a dozen women sat in a circle, our chairs close. First one and then the others spoke of their problems. When my turn came I simply opened my mouth and words tumbled out, telling as much as I could in the ten minutes we were each allotted. It was soon over; we all stood to leave, and the good doctor turned to me and asked me to stay. He said he wanted to talk to me.

I nodded my head and sat down, my heart pounding. I was thinking, "I have finally found someone who knows and understands. He's going to tell me where to go to get the help I so desperately need… because I'm crazy."

So you can imagine my shock when he told me he'd been so impressed by my awareness of my feelings that he wanted me to lead my own group for divorced women!

That was all I needed. I thanked him for sharing his observation with me. He'd just told me it was normal to have the feelings and thoughts I'd been having after going through two bad divorces. I was sane, after all.

I thanked him again for his confidence in me, but told him I wouldn't be back to lead a group.

I had a new life to live, and I was going to go out and live it.

30. Teeters Plastic Floral Products
1974

When Jerry and I divorced, a lot of people assumed I got a big settlement. Seeing that I'd always handled the money during our marriage, I knew there was no big settlement to be had. So when the judge decreed that he had to pay me $250,000 I was the one who suggested it be spread out over five years. I knew that was my only chance of getting a dime. Little did I know at the time I'd have to fight him in court every year to get that $50,000 and that by the last year I'd just give up. But that's another story.

I also got two of our seven or eight cars, a set of dishes, and a clock.

Jerry complained that I'd taken the clock.

And there certainly wasn't any kind of settlement from Pete.

There I was, twenty-nine years old, having been a wife for over fifteen years. I hadn't gone to high school. In fact, I'd pretty much just lived in a world where reality doesn't dwell.

Job options were limited. And I needed one.

When I got a job as a receptionist in a warehouse called Teeters that sold plastic flowers and plants, I was thrilled to earn $103.00 a week. It meant to me that I did have a "value." Not a lot, but still value. This was my new beginning.

I had to laugh later about my job interview. My potential new boss asked me to type a letter, and handed me two sheets of paper and a sheet of carbon paper. My heart leaped into my throat. What would I do if I put it together backwards? I arranged the three sheets, laid them on the corner of the desk and made a small scratch with my fingernail. Luck was with me; I had it right.

But it turned out that my devotion to plastic floral products wilted quickly. It wasn't long before I was bored silly. So I got a job at ABC Southeastern Theatres, Inc., a company that calculated the money due to movie studios from theaters. It was a numbers job and I liked it. My task of making sure every penny added up correctly was challenging, which was just what I needed.

During that job I had one of those days that most people have had at some point. Things had been going wrong for days. My divorce to Pete had run into some nasty snags and Jerry was being difficult, as usual. I went to work each day glad to focus on numbers instead of the men in my life. I tried hard that particular day to push my troubles out of my head but they kept rumbling back in. Then I absently picked up a pen to jot down a number and that stupid pen wouldn't write. That was the last straw. I started to sob. And sob. Coworkers had to help me into the bathroom so I could calm down.

Sometimes it's the little things.

Before too long, encouraged by my daddy, I took a real estate class. Daddy assured me that I could indeed sell real estate and I never doubted his judgment. He was right. Selling real estate is a problem-solving job. Never have I met any client who put more demands on me than my first ex-husband. I never thought of it as "training," but after what I went through in that marriage, negotiating a contract over a house is a piece of cake. Motivated to learn, I got my GED, took the required classes, and became a licensed real estate agent. I am now a real estate broker.

The real estate business has been very good to me, and I have loved the work and the challenge. Through the business I met the kind, stable, loving, successful businessman I eventually married. We've been together for over thirty years. He's nothing like a rock-and-roll star. Thank goodness!!

I'm living proof that your past does not have to determine your present, or your future, for that matter. If you feel like nothing, that means you have the freedom to make yourself anything you want to be. As I always say, if a naïve thirteen-year-old girl could elope with her famous second cousin, and survive all of the tragedy and trouble that wrought, you can survive your dumbass decisions, too.

31. **The Million Dollar Club** | 1980

I owe a lot of my real estate success to Jerry. I'm not even being sarcastic.

Hear me out and you'll understand.

Real estate is a problem-solving job. If you lose your head when things go wrong, you won't last. You cannot let yourself become part of the problem, as my broker used to say, but rather must solve problems.

When I first heard those words I felt at home. I'd been training for this job for years. I'd taught myself to turn myself inside out to keep Jerry happy, as a good wife was supposed to do. Don't become part of the problem. Just solve it. Period.

My gut instinct was to do business that way and it worked. It still does. When things get crazy I get calm. This is my game. The same principles applied and I'd perfected them. Real estate was a breath of fresh air. I knew that if I could get Jerry Lee Lewis to calm down—something I'd become very adept at—I could get anyone to calm down. That works in business and it works in life. I could have looked the world over and never found another line of work I was more suited for. It fit me like a custom-made $1000 suit.

Right from the start I truly enjoyed helping my clients solve the problem of finding a home that was just right for them. When things went too smoothly I admit I was a little disappointed. I was up to the fight and felt a bit let down when it didn't happen. In my experience, life just wasn't supposed to be that easy.

Once I was confident that I had all of the knowledge I needed to represent a client, I soared like an eagle. I loved the business and I loved my clients. The first three years I'd cry after a closing because they no longer needed me. Our time together had ended and it made me sad. I had formed an attachment to them, solving whatever problems came our way in the process of home buying and now it was over.

I made some great friends and met people from all walks of life. Most had no idea I had been the child bride of "the Killer." Once in a great while I'd even overhear a client refer to Jerry Lee Lewis or to my book, *Great Balls of Fire*, published in 1982, and the subsequent movie with Winona Ryder and Dennis Quaid. I wouldn't say a word.

I sold one family's home and then sold them a new home. Years later the husband called me and said he had a funny story to tell me. He'd seen a woman on TV who looked and sounded just like me. Her name was "…of all things, Myra."

When I said, "That was me," he called out to his wife and said, "That *was* our Myra!"

There is another client I'll never forget. While we rode around in my car, looking at house after house, he told me a bit of his life story. It turned out he'd been stationed at the same Army base in North Carolina where my first cousin, Major James Henry Merrill had died in a freak plane crash a number of years earlier. I asked if he had by chance known Jim.

He said, "Yes, I knew him. I was at his funeral and will never forget when they played the song *Dixie*."

At the mention of that song I had to pull off the road,

I was crying so hard. He started crying, too. To this day, I have never been able to tell this story without crying. It meant the world to me to know that this man had felt admiration for my cousin, who I'd adored. When we were kids he was my best playmate and favorite person in the world.

My client swiped at his tears and said, "We loved him, too."

~

"I wish I was in the land of cotton, old times there are not forgotten, look away, look away, look away Dixie Land."

Dixie Land has been good to me. My adopted home of Atlanta—I've lived in Duluth just outside of Atlanta for many years now—turned out to be a perfect landing place for rebuilding my life professionally as well as personally. I've won many sales awards and have been a member of what they call "the Million Dollar Club" for a long time. I've made a good living at real estate, enough that when times get bad I can carry on.

Sometimes I think of retiring, but a new client or old friend comes along who wants to sell or buy a house, and there I am in my car again, solving that problem of finding the perfect home for someone who is moving on with their life. I can't think of any other kind of work I'd rather do.

32. **And Then There was Richard** | 1980

I had never had a man who opened a car door for me. I didn't know there were men out there like that. I thought the new "lifestyles" had made us all on the same level. If so, no one told Richard Williams.

I had never been on a pedestal before, either, or treated like a princess. I had no idea it could be so enchanting, not until Richard came along and swept me off my feet.

We've been married for over thirty years and he is still a true gentleman in every sense of the word. When we have dinner he will stand and wait for me to be seated. He treats me like I mean the world to him. Best of all, I know I do.

No, I was not accustomed to being treated with such love and respect by a man I was with, but I will take it. I will take all of it I can get.

I met Richard when he interviewed me to work in his office. It was 1980 and I was a green-as-grass realtor. He was a real estate broker with his own company and I wanted to work there. At first I was so intimidated by him and his knowledge, I could hardly speak to him. I thought he knew everything in that business. (And he just about does.) I admired him from day one.

I worked in his office for four years before he asked me to lunch.

Falling in love with Richard was an easy thing to do. He's a soft-spoken gentleman who never raises his voice.

Back then he wore a suit and a tie every day. He opened doors for ladies and stood until they were seated, and still does those considerate things today. He's at ease in any situation, talking to anyone. It doesn't matter if it's business or casual. I like that in a man. He's comfortable with himself and makes others around him feel comfortable, too.

And he's certainly one of the best businessmen I've ever met.

I confess, it doesn't hurt that he's good looking, too.

I'd been single for almost thirteen years by the time he asked me out. I'd dated on occasion. However, I'd never met anyone I would consider marrying. Seems like they all wanted to marry me, though. I kept running into men who were looking for a trophy, you-know-who's ex-wife. That was the absolute last thing I wanted.

After all I'd been through I needed real love and a real man who would be there for me.

That was Richard. He didn't care whose ex-wife I was. All he cared about was me. I didn't hesitate to say "yes" when he asked me to be his wife.

We were married in a train station in June, 1984. Yes, a *train station* in Tucker, Georgia. It's an old historic building and seemed just right for the small affair we had planned. It was a Friday and, unfortunately, that afternoon I had a closing on a house that had more problems than usual. After such a long delay the attorney apologized and said he knew we all had better places to be. A few grumbled and I spoke up. "I'm supposed to be getting married this afternoon!" The attorney laughed, until I said, "I am not kidding."

Everybody was flabbergasted. But I explained that my intended was my boss and he'd understand.

Finally, all the right papers arrived and were signed, and I walked out the door at twenty minutes to 5:00, thinking if I could just make it through traffic to get to the train station by 5:00 I'd have it made. The wedding party, a few friends and family and Richard, were standing outside when I drove up. I ran from the car to the station. The Justice of the Peace had locked up and was about to leave, but Richard detained him until I could get to the door. We pled our case; it didn't take much for him to unlock the door. We all scurried inside and took our positions. It was a very short, "Do you take...?" and "Do you take...?"

"Yes," "Yes," we said.

We went to a local restaurant and celebrated at last. They brought out a wedding cake and on it was written "It's About Time." That was 1984 but I swear it seems like just ten years ago.

That's a happy life, when you lose count of the years and thirty feels like ten.

Today my husband is still fit, especially for a man in his seventies. He's an avid golfer. We belong to a club where he plays regularly and belongs to a poker group. He loves doing "guy stuff."

One of Richard's proudest accomplishments was serving his country in the U.S. Army Security Agency for three years. He spent two years in Europe where he made an all-service basketball team that defeated all of the Olympic teams in Western Europe. In Istanbul, Turkey, he played in the CISM (Conseil International du sport Militaire) military world games, defeating the Turkish team in the championship finals. He enjoyed playing the Polish Olympic team in Brussels, Belgium, on New Year's Eve, 1960.

Richard loved playing basketball to entertain our military troops.

Today I leave him alone while he enjoys his sports and he leaves me alone when I shop at Goodwill, at a consignment store, or on QVC. No matter how much money I have, I've never been a big spender. I grew up watching my parents count their pennies and that's what I've always done. Richard is an excellent financial planner, so we get along well when it comes to the one thing so many couples fight about. Neither of us is a spendthrift.

His patience shows when he helps me in the garden or the house. I love to garden and am forever needing more dirt and moving plants around. Richard tolerates it all and simply moves whatever I want to wherever I want it. And then moves it again when I change my mind.

It's the same in the house. I love rearranging, and he has never complained.

We have the nice, cozy home I always dreamed of, and I even included a white picket fence. We have dogs and are the kind of dog parents who treat them like children. They are our babies.

I'm reminded of what a good man I'm married to every time Richard walks through the door and our dogs go berserk with joy. Dogs know. This is a man to be loved.

I love him with all my heart and thank the dear Lord every day that I finally found the man of my dreams.

33. Making a Movie: *Great Balls of Fire!* | 1989

It took five years to accurately put together the information for my book *Great Balls of Fire*. Murray Silver, the co-writer, estimated it would take six months. Not only did it take much longer than expected, it certainly was not the book I had started out to write. I wanted it to be a woman's story of survival, just like this book is. However, the publisher in NYC had other ideas. They point blank said, "Nobody wants to read the ex-wife's story. They want to read about Jerry Lee Lewis!"

Fine. This threw me off track and sent Murray into a frantic search for the actual dates of performances. No, not at all the book I wanted to write.

It was finally published in 1989.

Then Hollywood became interested but rather than deal with just me, the rightful owner of the book, they wanted J.L.L. involved. Good luck. Have you heard the saying "screw up a two car funeral?" Making the movie became more difficult on a daily basis.

Finally Dennis Quaid was cast as Jerry and Winona Ryder played me. Filming began and I went to Memphis, where some of the filming took place, to visit the set.

Dennis, either on his own or because that was what he was directed to do, portrayed Jerry as a total goofball. Oh, please. "Beam me up, Scotty," I thought. "There's no intelligent life on this set."

One day after watching a scene I went to the director and said, "Excuse me, but that scene didn't happen that way."

He said, "Well, if it didn't it should have, and maybe it will next time."

That's a definition of the truth I had not heard before. The very next day I was on the set again, and was shown the set of our house and my bedroom. They had gone to great lengths to get items from the early '50s. However, a quick drive out to Coro Lake and a look at the real house I grew up in would have given them a ton of information about what it really looked like. When I saw what they turned our home into on the set I sat down and cried. The set designer was upset, too. They had a wood-sided house in a cheap neighborhood. In reality our house was a brick ranch style on a slight hill overlooking a lake. They had shabby, cheap, old furniture and tasteless décor. The truth was my dad had a good job with the power company and my mom had (and still has) great taste. We weren't rich but we weren't poor, either. The way they depicted our home didn't give credit to my daddy for working hard and providing well for us or to my momma for keeping a nice, comfy home.

But they did find a box of Kleenex that was the actual size of Kleenex back then. You'd be amazed at how much it's shrunk over the years. At least they got that right.

The producers wanted promotional photographs with the cast. Winona Ryder was very sweet. But Dennis Quaid wouldn't have spit on me if I was on fire.

Once the photo shoot was over, I could tell it was time for me to take my crying eyes back to Georgia. So I went home, never to return to the set again.

I saw the movie once. Once was enough.

34. If Larry Oliver Calls, Tell Him I'm Out | 1989

Not long after *Great Balls of Fire,* the movie, was released I was asked to appear on "The Merv Griffin Show." It was 1989 and that was one of the most popular shows on TV at the time, so I was happy to oblige. The network flew me to L.A., had me picked up in a limo, and had the driver deliver me to the Studio. It was well after 9 p.m. in Hollywood when I arrived for the nighttime show.

I walked in the backdoor and there was no one backstage. The stagehands, apparently, had gone for the day, along with everyone else, including the producer and crew. There was silence everywhere. The halls were as quiet as a tomb.

The limo driver took my bags to one of the backstage "green rooms" where I sat for a good twenty minutes before venturing out on my own. I walked the darkened, silent halls. This was nothing like the other TV shows I had appeared on, like Phil Donahue and Sally Jessy Raphael, which made me even more curious about this one.

I came upon a room that had lights on. Inside one lone man was getting makeup put on for his appearance on the show. At last I'd found someone to talk to.

"Hello!" I called to the two men, the one applying the makeup, and the other reclined and relaxed. "This place is so quiet, where did everyone go?" I said as I climbed into the makeup chair beside them. I sat swinging my chair from side to side and asked the guy being made up, "So you're going to be on the show tonight, huh?"

"Yes, I am," he replied in a deep mellow voice with a British accent.

"Yeah, me too," I said. I stayed a few more minutes and chatted but the conversation quickly died, so I stood up and started for the door. "Good luck!" I said. "It was nice talking to you."

I went back to my dressing room and watched the show on one of the monitors. The gentleman I'd met earlier was now sitting in the guest chair next to Merv's desk and they were conversing about something that I didn't really catch. Merv called the man by name: Larry. You could tell they had been friends for years as they laughed and told funnies that happened when they were together.

Larry and Merv finished, Larry left the stage, and it was my turn. I walked onstage in front of the cameras and was introduced. I went over and sat in the chair where Larry had been sitting.

I don't remember the exact questions Merv asked me. However, most of my interviews were all about the same. What was it like to be the child bride of Jerry Lee Lewis? What made me want to write a book about it?

When the questions were done, Merv thanked me for being his guest. I stood, shook his hand, the audience applauded, and I walked away stage right. It turned out, however, I was supposed to leave stage *left*. I pulled the curtain back and was met by a brick wall. I stepped behind the curtain, pulled it shut, and just stood there until a kindhearted stagehand fetched me to lead me back across the stage. That took me back between Merv and the cameras so I gave the audience a second wave goodbye and, what the hell, I added a curtsy.

When I arrived back home in Atlanta I talked to my book's co-writer, Murray Silver. He asked who was on the show with me. I told him a guy named Larry. I didn't know what he did or who he was except that Merv called him Larry and they kept running a name on the screen that I thought was Oliver. But I didn't know who Larry Oliver was.

Murray repeated the name "Larry Oliver" a few times, then with a gasp he said, "Myra, was it Sir Lawrence Olivier, one of the greatest actors in the entire world?"

"Yes!" I said. "They did have 'Sir' in front of his name. That must have been who that was."

This was one trip I wished I had not made. I made a fool of myself in front of Sir Lawrence Olivier, then I walked into a brick wall and had to be rescued, and then I proved to the audience how stupid I was by giving them a curtsy like a five-year-old. I'll bet the audience left that night saying. "I can't believe Jerry Lee Lewis married that stupid girl. I thought he was smarter than that."

35. **The Standoff** | 1999

Jerry Lee was on drugs and on his sixth wife when Phoebe got a call from the wife, Kerrie. She told Phoebe she was divorcing Jerry and unless Phoebe wanted him to be alone, which was a bad idea, she'd better get to the farm ASAP.

Phoebe was living in Nashville, pursuing a singing career. Moving to a farm in Mississippi wasn't on her immediate agenda, but she'd always known this call might come one day and she had long since made up her mind that if her daddy needed her she would be there. She just hadn't known how long it would take.

She told her roommate in Nashville that she would be back before long and that she'd send rent money in the meantime. With a few changes of clothes, she left for what she thought would be a short trip.

She ended up sending rent money for a full year and eventually went back to retrieve her belongings. But she never retrieved her life in Nashville.

Jerry spent his days in bed watching reruns of *Gunsmoke*, taking pills to go to sleep, and pills to wake up. He expected food to be brought into him on a tray. Once in a while he managed to go to the kitchen for a Coke, if his hollering for one didn't get a response.

Housekeeping had apparently not been on Kerrie's list of things to do. She'd been the worst housekeeper in the world. The house was a wreck—and it stunk.

Kerrie had left a herd of Chihuahua dogs in her wake

and none had been house-trained. They would just pee and poop wherever they wanted, and the carpets were soaked in dog urine all the way through the pads. I was visiting Phoebe once while Kerrie was still there and a dog peed right in front of us. Kerry just took her big foot and ground it into the carpet, as if that would take care of it. The resulting smell of all that mess was unbearable but I guess some people get used to it over time. The fact that those poor dogs were neither spayed nor neutered caused another set of problems.

One night, Phoebe woke up in the middle of the night and decided she couldn't stand it for one more minute. She was sick and tired of burrowing into the blankets to try to stem the stench of dog urine. Throwing back the covers, she got up and went to work cutting the carpet out of the guest room, which was now hers. She dragged that smelly mess outside and heaved it onto the lawn. Then she scrubbed the subflooring with water and bleach again and again.

The hall carpet was next to go. And then the rest of the house.

And wouldn't you know that about that time Kerrie changed her mind. She didn't want a divorce after all. She came back.

The time that I visited Phoebe I couldn't believe my eyes at what Kerrie had done to that house. What had once been a nice home, designed by a prominent Memphis contractor, on thirty-two acres overlooking a private lake, had become a temple of tacky. First of all, she'd decorated with fake gold all over the place. Gold furniture, gold pillows, gold crap. Even the beautiful wood paneling had been spray painted gold. She was out of control. The spray can decorating had become so feverish she even painted the baby grand piano I'd given Jerry during our marriage. It was now crackle gold.

Her dream home. She even outfitted Jerry in a gold jacket to match her color scheme.

Kerrie had called Phoebe to come take care of her dad but then decided to reappear and shack up in the garage apartment. Then she hauled her bed from the apartment to the den of the main house so she could set roots for what would become a long, ridiculous fight. She relocated the herd of Chihuahuas to her bed/den and began a campaign of intimidation which Phoebe at the time was able to counter. Within a few days she disappeared again for a couple of weeks, abandoning her Chihuahuas yet again in a room full of dog shit. This became a pattern.

Jerry stayed in his room, which he'd fortified with a huge, locked, wrought iron door. A Sherman tank couldn't knock that thing down nor, as Phoebe called her, could the S.S. Kerrie. Phoebe would hole up in her room not knowing when Kerrie would appear out of nowhere. It was a stand-off, a war, and Phoebe was determined to win it. But, so was Kerrie. She wasn't going to back down, either.

One day Kerrie came to Phoebe and tossed a huge stack of unpaid bills at her, and said, "Here, Bitch, you want it, you got it!" Maybe she thought that would be a sure-fire way to get rid of her step-daughter, once it was revealed that there was obviously very little of Jerry's money left. But realizing that her daddy had no financial security made Phoebe all the more resolved to get him back on track, physically and financially. This was a pivotal moment and Phoebe dug in for the hellacious divorce which was to follow.

The divorce dragged on for five long years. An armed guard was hired to sit in the living room because Jerry's attorney feared for Phoebe's life. Kerrie only left the house after the divorce was final and the judge set a date for her to be off of the property with all of her golden shit. It took a sheriff to force her to leave at the final hour.

By the time the divorce went to court for a final decree, Kerrie had a baby girl named Star Lee. She'd also had a son earlier in their marriage, Jerry Lee Lewis, III. The court ordered DNA tests. To my knowledge, Kerrie never even bothered having Star Lee tested. I guess it's hard to make a baby through a locked wrought iron door. As for Jerry Lee, III, the test proved that he is not Jerry's biological child. Nobody to date has managed to pass the DNA tests, making Phoebe Jerry Lee Lewis' only living biological child. But Jerry was there when Jerry Lee, III, was born and grew up. Jerry loves boys and loves this child as if he were his own.

Phoebe's "visit" to her dad's farm lasted twelve years. Longer than some of his marriages.

36. **Déjà vu All Over Again** | 1999

I wish I could say that the troubles end, but the truth is they don't always. We just learn to deal with them.

When my daughter, Phoebe, became her daddy's business manager, I feared for what was to come. Other parents undoubtedly have experienced what I went through at that time. After the stress I had endured in my relationship with the man, it was disturbing to know that my child was about to become embroiled in the same chaotic lifestyle. As parents, when we see our grown-up child headed in a direction that makes us afraid for them, we want to grab them, lock them in their room, and tell them they are grounded. Of course, we can't do that.

Early in this venture my parents and I went to visit her. She was already working non-stop, on the phone, taking care of business, and solving problems. There was no slowdown; the merry-go-round was already spinning. As we pulled out of the driveway to return home to Atlanta, where my parents now live, too, with Daddy driving, Mom in front, and me in the backseat—I know, just like when I was a kid—I turned to see my child waving goodbye, and I became overwhelmed with a need to throw my arms around her and protect her. The impulse was so crushing I couldn't breathe! I heard a scream, "Stop, Daddy, Stop!" Daddy slammed on the brakes, and I jumped out and ran to my daughter. We held each other and cried. When our car finally drove away with me in it, it was one of the most difficult partings of my life.

I knew that she would be working with a man who is out of touch with reality—he doesn't live in reality and reality doesn't live in him—and that it would exhaust her mentally, physically, and emotionally. That's what it had done to me. Even though I was only thirteen when we married, I picked up where his momma left off. I waited on him hand and foot. For example, he never ate a meal at the dinner table. I brought a tray that fit perfectly over the arms of his big leather chair and served every single meal to him. Jerry was not used to making decisions; he expected someone to take care of everything.

This was a lesson I learned very early in our marriage when he bought a new convertible Ford. Late one night a man knocked on our door and wanted the payments that were three months behind. He was from the finance company. I couldn't believe my eyes that Jerry never thought about paying bills. My parents were meticulous about this so I thought everyone was. From that night on I took over, paying all of the bills and taking care of the business affairs of our family. I made deposits in the bank, wrote checks, and simply managed everything, even the decisions. Jerry wanted no part of any of it.

I knew Phoebe would have her own obstacles working with Jerry. She ended up living on his farm for twelve years serving as business manager, accountant, travel guide, tax advisor, cook, chauffeur, maid, and life-saver!

But because of her hard work from dawn 'til dusk; making phone calls, booking events, scheduling private planes, and so much more; Jerry's career took off again. Just when some considered "the Killer" to be a has-been, his career broke records. Phoebe was physically and mentally exhausted, but it was worth it to her. They were really on a roll.

Jerry Lee Lewis was a rock-and-roll force to be reckoned with once again.

What could possibly go wrong?

37. Fake Balls Of Fire | 2001

The gun was placed close to the woman's head, the trigger pulled. The bullet struck her just below her right ear, killing her instantly. Dead was one woman with a scheming, solitary goal: to catch a rich, famous husband. This woman had reached her goal; she had caught the brass ring. She had married famous actor Robert Blake and given birth to a daughter proven to be his.

She captured him as a hunter stalks her prey. I say this because she had tried but failed to capture others. One of those others was Jerry Lee Lewis.

Now it was May 4, 2001, Los Angeles, California, and Bonnie Lee Bakley was no more, slumped in the front seat of a car as her blood pooled beneath her.

The worst part of this tragedy was that her eleven-month-old child, her daughter with Robert Blake, was left behind.

Years earlier, Bonnie had given birth to a baby girl who she named Jeri Lee Lewis. It was an obvious attempt to capture the man Jerry Lee Lewis. But this was not a trick that worked every time. After years of chasing him without success—with Jerry it was like trying to shoot at a moving target—she moved on.

It's sad to think that any woman would be so desperate or self-absorbed, or whatever it was that she was, that she would stoop to such a level to try to get a man. Unfortunately, there are too many such women around. Famous men, rich men, and I suppose even very handsome men have to constantly watch over their shoulders for these vipers who offer them fake love.

But Jerry Lee, a lot older and not nearly as nimble as he used to be, seems especially vulnerable to me. He's easier prey.

Today I fear he has been caught.

38. **Fighting Baby Huey** | 2005

Over the years Jerry and I had fallen into a neutral relationship, like so many divorced parents who share a child. We were on pretty good speaking terms. In fact, I'd say that when we weren't fighting, we were actually friends.

That continued, for the most part, while Phoebe worked with him. Because she was always working, the only way I could visit her was to go to the farm. Jerry and I usually did a decent job of avoiding each other. For example, I'd clean something in the kitchen while waiting for her to get done working so we could go to dinner. He'd stay in his bedroom, watching *Gunsmoke* on television. He's watched so much of that show his brain has turned into *Gunsmoke* jelly by now.

There was one beautiful spring day when I went out to the patio with a broom to sweep away the leaves. Phoebe came running over to me and said, "Mother, I can't find Topaz! Go in there and see if he's with Daddy! Daddy will die if we let his dog get out and it runs away!"

So, I walked down the hall and went into Jerry's room where he lay propped up in his bed on three pillows with an unlit pipe clenched in his teeth, watching another rerun of *Gunsmoke*. I stopped at the foot of his bed and he glanced up at me with a questioning look on his face.

"Jerry," I said, "is Topaz in here with you?"

"No," he quipped and turned back to his show.

I ran out to Phoebe and said, "He's not in there."

Busy trying to get something else done, she looked

around and said, "Mother, go back and ask him again. He's got to be there."

Once again I took my flip-flops down the hall and into Jerry's room, and asked again, "Jerry, are you sure Topaz is not in here?"

He took the pipe from his clenched teeth and said, "Have ya'll lost my dog?" in a very sarcastic tone.

To which I put my hands on my hips and answered with my own mocking tone. "No we have not lost your dog." For a few seconds we glared at each other and as I turned to leave something under the cover at the foot of his bed started to move...ever so slightly. We both saw it at the same time and our eyes met.

"So-o-o-o," I said, "you didn't know where Topaz was, huh? Sure you didn't." And I whirled around and stomped out of his room.

He yelled out to me, "Hey, Girl, I didn't know he was in this bed! Did you hear me?" he yelled.

I just kept walking. I was more relieved than mad but I wasn't going to let him know that. When I reached the patio I told Phoebe, "Yes, he *was* in there," and I picked up the broom and returned to my sweeping. It was such a beautiful spring day....

Suddenly the glass door flew open and there he stood, decked out in nothing but his whitey-tighties. Now that is a sight no one ever needs to see. He reminded me of the cartoon character Baby Huey, the duck in a diaper. And Jerry was mad as a wet hen! Phoebe and I both turned to look at him at the same time, then we looked at each other as if to say, "What in the world is going on?"

Jerry yelled out to me, "Girl, are you calling me a liar?" I knew he was talking to me; he always called me "Girl."

"Well," I said, just as ornery as he had, "what do you think?"

"You'd better not call me..." he snarled back to me.

But before he could get it all said, Phoebe appeared in his face and said, "Daddy, go back to bed."

He looked at her and yelled, "Yo Momma done called me a liar!" and he started looking around for a weapon. But the only thing between me and him was a curled up water hose, still connected to the house, so he picked up the end of it and shook it around in my direction. Well, you can just picture what that looked like to me, with him holding that bit of limp hose in front of him. I was so unimpressed he became even more furious and threw it at me. It landed with a thud at his feet as he looked down at it in disgust.

To keep from laughing hysterically I started swinging my broom in the air over my head, making noises like a witch, just making sure he knew that if he threw that hose at me I would whack him with my broom. And then fly away on it!!!

I'd taken years of his yelling and my obeying, of his hitting and shoving and my cowering, and of being treated like dirt when we were married. I'd always swept it under the rug. So flipping up my broom and threatening to beat him over the head was one liberating moment! He ran back into the house as Phoebe and I fell into fits of laughter, wondering where those tabloid photographers were when you need them. That would have been one amazing photo-op!

39. The *Rolling Stone Magazine* Photo Shoot | 2006

The last time I saw Jerry Lee Lewis was at a photo shoot in 2006 for *Rolling Stone Magazine.* For some unknown reason the magazine thought it would be a good idea to photograph Jerry and me together.

Phoebe called me and stammered around trying to ask me something she obviously dreaded asking. At last she said, "Would you mind coming to see me and having your photo taken with my daddy?" She explained that the photo shoot was scheduled for a few weeks away. I said, "Of course, I'd be happy to. But whose idea is this?"

"It's *Rolling Stone Magazine's* idea," she said.

Wonderful. I didn't care who wanted my picture; I would get to see Phoebe for a few days. No problem here.

I made the trip and arrived the night before the shoot. It was scheduled for 11 a.m. the following morning. As a sweet gesture Phoebe had made arrangements, unbeknownst to me, for a pro to do my makeup and another pro to style my hair.

The moment I met the writer that morning he started doing an interview with me. He said they had a three o'clock plane to catch, which meant, "we gotta get the show on the road." I sat down in the dining room and we started talking. The makeup artist came over and started on my makeup right then and there. The writer and I talked a few minutes, and I noticed he was looking at me rather strangely. Finally he said, "Is that how you usually wear your makeup?"

"What?" I said. Someone handed me a mirror and, to my horror, Elvira looked back at me. I swear, I looked like a French whore. By then the makeup artist was desperately trying to get the blackest black off my eyes, which only managed to make it look like I had two big black eyes. The hairdresser was ready to start on my hair, hot curling iron in hand. The writer and I tried to ignore them and finish the interview. Then Phoebe came in and did a double take. I knew this was not good. Something told me that once again I wasn't gonna like what I saw. I stepped into the hall bathroom and almost fainted when I saw that the hairstylist had straightened both sides of my hair as if I had a wing going to the right and a wing going to the left, with a part down the middle.

This was a nightmare. In the next room was a bevy of photographers who were waiting to capture this on film! I grabbed my faithful curling iron, trying to make myself look less like the wicked witch. Now they were calling for me to come so they could start taking photos. Even Jerry was waiting on me.

There was no time for me to correct this atrocity, so the only thing I could do was to just mess up my hair and pray it appeared to be "just a casual 'do'."

They must have taken 250 pictures. At last they finished and off they went to the airport with photos of me that I would gladly have paid them any price to destroy.

Several weeks later Phoebe called and I could tell that once again she was dreading telling me something. Finally she gathered the courage to spit it out: They had decided not to use any of the photos I was in, but instead one lonely photo of Jerry by himself. I started shouting how wonderful that was. Phoebe couldn't believe I wasn't mad, especially after having driven all that way round trip from Atlanta. They weren't going to use any photos of me and I was ecstatic about it.

Those horrible photos of me wouldn't be seen and I got to see my girl. That was a good trip for me.

40. **Don't Shoot the Piano Player, Let Me** | 2011

I can't believe how it all came about. Phoebe had built up her daddy's business to the point that she was so overworked we all felt like she needed help. So my brother Rusty had a great idea! Since his wife of twenty-four years, Judith, wasn't working, she could go help out temporarily. We all breathed a sigh of relief; it was so wonderful to know that Phoebe had help. Then I suggested that Phoebe take Judith with them to go on a New York City media tour doing TV shows like *The View*, seeing that there would be a lot to do. Little did I know this would be the worst idea I ever had in my entire life. It was a humdinger!

It was on that trip that Judith got a glimpse of life in the limelight and she apparently really liked it. They traveled in a private jet, were picked up in a stretch limo, stayed at a fancy hotel, and were treated like royalty.

Next thing we knew, Judith divorced Rusty and married Jerry. She and Rusty had ups and downs over the course of their marriage, but Rusty always forgave her and moved on. For example, he told me about sitting beside her in court one day when she'd sued someone over an accident. Rusty was shocked and embarrassed when the defense attorney brought out a big white poster board with all of Judith's other lawsuits. Rusty had no idea she had a history of suing people. But he forgave his wife and moved on with their marriage.

Remember, Jerry had known Rusty since he was three years old and was Rusty's second cousin and ex-brother-in-law. Once he was old enough, Rusty played drums in Jerry's band for years. But never mind any of that; Jerry had once again selected a wife from amongst family. After all this family has been through, I don't know why some of us never dreamed that something like this could happen. Friends and other family members have since told us they were not surprised, but the immediate family was blindsided.

Jerry does like to keep it in the family, doesn't he?

The chaos continued as Phoebe was released of her duties. She moved away from the farm but was still under contract with her daddy. She also had a contract with Judith, her employee, as to what Judith could and could not do. So she was surprised when I called her telling her a cousin in Louisiana had called me and said Jerry was in the hospital there. What we found out was that Judith and Jerry had left the farm and rented a house in Natchez, Mississippi.

Curious, I called the Natchez courthouse and a very helpful woman who knew Jerry told me that he had recently been pushed in a wheelchair into the courthouse to apply for a marriage license. She said he didn't remember her and she thought he was totally out of it. She suspected drugs.

Now I was even more curious, so I called the biggest Baptist church in Natchez and lo-and-behold I got the preacher, who told me that Judith had asked him to perform a marriage ceremony for her and Jerry. The preacher expressed concern that he hadn't been able to talk to Jerry. He even told me that he'd stopped by the house a number of times and Judith had always told him that Jerry was either sleeping or didn't feel well. The preacher's concern was over his own rule of never marrying a couple without consulting with them individually first. He was very candid about his discomfort over breaking his own rule.

However, according to news reports the preacher did marry them in their own house. There were others present, and according to Rick Bragg's biography *Jerry Lee Lewis, My Story* Jerry said of the ceremony, "They kind of 'hemmed me in.' I felt bushwhacked… the preacher came in and they all started singing hymns."

I couldn't help but think that, yeah, he was bushwhacked but he let it happen because he was in desperate need of a handmaid. That's so Jerry.

You see, Phoebe had met the love of her life and planned on getting married.

But I must admit I'm concerned for Jerry. It's crossed my mind that he's worth more to his new wife dead than he is alive. It also appears that Judith is isolating her husband from some people in the family. For example, within a few days of the wedding, Phoebe's contract with her daddy was rescinded and the code on the gate to the farm had been changed, so Phoebe couldn't get in.

Phoebe has taken the high road and simply moved on with her life. Now she and her husband have a lovely, comfy home and relaxed lifestyle; they adore their dogs; and they work at their careers. When I drive away after a visit there are tears of joy, I'm so happy for her.

I guess I'd be surprised if things ever calmed down in the Jerry Lee Lewis camp. I'm just grateful every day that I've built a new life for myself; far, far away from the piano player who stole my innocence when I was still a child. One thing I know beyond a doubt… nothing will ever take me to the edge of emotional devastation again. I have been there. I know the pain. I will, with the help and power of God, survive whatever may come my way. There are no places lower than the places I have already been in my life.

Great balls of fire? For me, a tiny spark survived, a spark that turned out to be pretty darned good, if I say so myself. And that was all I needed to light the way to a better life.

41. Momma and Daddy's Rock-and-Roll Romance Today | 2015

This book wouldn't be complete without an update about my parent's rock-and-roll romance. It'll cheer you up after all of the stories about lying, cheating, divorce, death, and marrying within the family.

Lois and J.W. Brown are living proof that life-long love is possible.

At the time of this writing my parents are eighty-nine years old and are still in the prime of their lives. They have been married for over seventy-three years.

We still travel together just as we did when I was six years old. The backseat belongs to me. Just give me a coloring book and a new box of crayons and I become six again; except now, I bring a novel and read myself sleepy. Mom always tosses in a pillow and a quilt for me. With Daddy at the wheel I feel as safe as a baby wrapped in her momma's warm, cuddly arms.

A few years ago Mom and Daddy wanted my brother Rusty and me to take a road trip with them to visit family all throughout Louisiana, Mississippi, and Tennessee. Neither Rusty nor I relished the idea of traveling 1600 miles like that, but how could we say no? We know that at their age it could be our last such adventure together and the last time they would see some of those relatives. But my brother and I laugh at that idea, seeing that we can hardly keep up with our parents. They're always doing something and going somewhere, mostly to the casinos in Biloxi. We made the trip, and Rusty and I didn't even fight once like kids do on vacation with their parents.

One thing that trip did was remind us of the love our parents still have for each other. That really is miraculous. Rusty is divorced and I've been happily married to my husband Richard for thirty years. But my brother and I can't live long enough to make it to seventy years with a spouse like our parents have done.

To this day my mom still combs her hair and puts on lipstick every time her husband is about to come home. And to this day, his eyes light up every time he walks in that door and sees his wife.

I suspect that in their minds they are still sixteen years old. She's still that beautiful, dark-haired girl and he's that tall, handsome boy. They love each other today every bit as much as they did back then, and more.

Their rock-and-roll romance is here to stay.

42. **Thank You, J.W. Brown** | 2015

Only when I became an adult could I appreciate what an awful, impossible position my daddy had been thrown into when Jerry and I got married. The monkey wrench had been thrown into the works and J.W. lost his livelihood, all of his time and effort, and his dream of being back in the music business. Everything he had put forth on J.L.L.'s behalf was water under the bridge, long gone. Jerry resented anyone claiming credit for his success except the man himself. To hear him tell it, it was his talent and his talent alone that created his success. Nothing else had a damned thing to do with it.

Forget Daddy turning down the offer of a lifetime job with Memphis Light Gas and Water after his accident: an easy job and full retirement. He gave that up in order to throw all of his time and energy into launching a music career for J.L.L. and the band he would be part of. That, too, was water under the bridge. Daddy hadn't hesitated about giving up the job. He was part of the show; he was happy; and he was back where he always longed to be—in the music scene. His motto was the old, "There's no business like show business."

Once my daddy had gone back to Mississippi to find his cousin and coax him into coming to Memphis for an audition at Sun Records, he looked around and knew damned well that Jerry was going to be a star and contender for the number one position in this up-and-coming thing called rock-and-roll. J.W. also knew his own talent on the bass guitar was awesome, and he knew his way around a stage and the crowds. He knew how to work the scene. It was he who wired Jerry's piano with a violin amp so it would sound as if you were standing right in front of it.

But when I married Jerry Lee, my daddy was kicked back to square one. Here he was thirty-one years old and his teenaged daughter had shattered his dream. No way was he about to work for the man who had stolen his daughter right out from under him.

When Daddy invited his other cousin, Mickey Gilley, to travel to California with him and my mom in search of a recording contract for Mickey, that was seen by Jerry Lee as a direct attempt to undermine him. My Daddy never even considered anything like that. He just needed to make a living. And music was his first choice. But by the time my parents and Mickey went to California, Mickey was living in Houston, Texas, and had established himself there. Continuing to work with Mickey wouldn't have fit for our family that was rooted in Memphis, Tennessee.

So when Jerry would call his Memphis cousin to ask him to come back to work because he needed him, Daddy always relented and went. Every time Daddy would go back to work for Jerry, things would be great for a few weeks. Then something would happen that Jerry would get mad at Daddy, and J.L.L. would scream at him with things like, "You think you made me, don't you J.W.?" And off they would go into a harsh argument. Daddy quit and went back to work with Jerry so many times we all lost track.

Jerry and J.W. had an agreement in the beginning where they would be fifty-fifty partners. That lasted no time at all. Then Daddy was bumped down to twenty-five per cent.

Then the day came when Jerry told J.W. that he was going to pay him just like he was a side-man. Side-men were nothing special, they come and go, and are a dime a dozen. Jerry forgot what J.W. did for him, what no one had been able to accomplish. Or had the desire to.

That final cut was a converging of the perfect storm.

Daddy said, "No, you're not going to pay me at all, Jerry. I quit. I'll be damned if after all I have done for you, you want to demote me to pay like I'm a musician you'd pick up on a damn street corner."

That ended the job and a big part of the relationship. It broke my heart that my own husband had no concern for the man that did more to help him launch his career than anyone else on earth; much less did he care if he was his father-in-law. I was helpless to change any of it.

One thing I found out later was blown out of reason. In the beginning, Jerry and Daddy had formed a corporation. All of the money went into the corporation. Taxes were paid as they came due. Jerry and J.W. got their checks every week. The rest of the money was held in the corporation, like with any business that wants to operate successfully.

But Jerry made the mistake of having Lois, my mother, send a corporate check to his mother, Mamie. The crap hit the fan! Mamie told her son that those people were going to steal everything he had. She knew nothing about corporations. My mother handled the money and was bonded. Any disappearance of money would have landed her in jail. All Jerry's family had ever worked on was a sharecropping farm where his mother got her money when the cotton was sold. Yet she somehow made J.L.L. believe that the Browns were going to steal every penny he had.

How quickly she and her son forgot about how Jerry

had paid no rent or bought so much as a loaf of bread to contribute to meals for a year while he lived in my parents' house. My daddy drove his own car on their first tours. My daddy was the one who dug Jerry up in Mississippi, for goodness sake, and convinced him to come to Memphis. My daddy set up Jerry's first audition at Sun Records.

All forgotten.

Jerry told my parents, "the Browns," to dissolve the corporation and that he wanted all of his money right now. That was Jerry's first step to screwing up his finances and fighting with Uncle Sam for years and years to come.

My parents, on the other hand, have never been wealthy but have never had any trouble handling money responsibly. They wouldn't dream of letting a bill go unpaid. The day that a bill arrives in the mail they sit down and write a check to pay it. That check is back in the mail by the next day.

J. W. Brown: The man who deserves credit for Jerry's start in the music business was not only mistreated and fired but was denied recognition for what he did. Jerry will never acknowledge my daddy. Jerry's pride swells up and his head begins to believe his own lies. I wonder if in the silent dark of night J.L.L. ever thinks of this and feels any pangs of guilt. Somehow I think not. I wish it were different, but I know this will never change.

In spite of it all, my daddy worships the ground Jerry walks on. He reveres the man's talent. God bless J.W. Brown, one outstanding, talented man with a heart of gold. He played a pivotal role in J.L.L.'s career but has always been denied that he had any part in it.

The world may never know the truth but I know it, my Daddy knows it, and Jerry Lee Lewis knows it, too.

43. **We've Gotta Have Friends** | 1980-Now

One more part of my life that is important to me is my friends. When I was a kid I loved my friends. I had friends at school and in my neighborhood, but my favorite was my cousin, Jim Merrill.

He was a year older than me and he knew everything. He knew he was going to be the president of the United States when he grew up and I was going to Washington, D.C., with him as his personal secretary. That's how smart he was! Most of our days were spent in the "office" of Pop Merrill, Jim's daddy, who was a contractor for the state of Louisiana. His office was built behind his home on the back two acres. It had two full offices with big desks, chairs that whirled, and lots of big books on which to write. President Jim would instruct me what to write and I would make a squiggle in a book. Only I knew what it meant. It was code, ya know. Jim insisted his younger brothers salute him when they came for a visit. After all, the future president was not to be disrespected.

President Jim's daddy had a new concrete driveway poured at their home that summer and for a future president it was an excellent opportunity to go down in history. Jim signed his name in the wet cement: "Major James Henry Merrill." Oh, what a proud moment. I stood guard but didn't make a comment in the cement since I couldn't write yet. When Jim's Daddy saw the statement in his newly poured driveway, he didn't have to go far to find the perpetrator. But Jim didn't get in trouble; he was always so good.

When Jim grew up he attended the Citadel, graduated with honors, and joined the Vietnam War efforts flying a helicopter, rescuing the wounded. As I mentioned earlier, Jim died on American soil during a training mission when his plane crashed. At the time of his death he was "Major James Henry Merrill." I still miss him!

Jim left two young sons, one who is in politics in South Carolina, James Henry Merrill Jr. He's following in his father's footsteps.

Jim notwithstanding, my friendships pretty much ended, however, when I married Jerry Lee Lewis. Not too many parents want their thirteen-year-old daughters to be friends with a girl their age who is married. Besides, Jerry didn't want me to have friends. If I was talking to someone on the phone he always wanted to know who it was and would tell me to get off the phone. The few friends I had learned to call me when he was out of town on tour.

Now I relish my friendships. One friend I've had for many years is Brenda, a hairdresser I met after I'd divorced Jerry and moved to Georgia. Whenever I knew Jerry was doing a show near our home I'd take Phoebe so she could see her Daddy. The first time I met Brenda she was there cutting Jerry's hair. We quickly became fast friends. She was a fan of Jerry's and offered to cut his hair one night before he went on stage. He was thrilled. From then on she would cut his hair anytime he was anywhere near Atlanta. She even became my hairdresser for years.

She did other celebrities' hair, too, and always has fun

stories to tell. Her family background with its deep Southern roots is fascinating, as well as the fact that she's a distant cousin of the late actress Evelyn Keyes, Scarlett's sister in *Gone with the Wind.* You cannot get any more Southern than that.

A woman I met years ago at work who became a good friend is named Lin. We have what many would call an unusual connection. We immediately felt like we'd known each other for years, almost as if we'd been friends or relatives before. I believe in past lives and suspect we were sisters in another lifetime. Then her husband was transferred and they moved away. When she left I cried at the mention of her name. I could not even talk about her without crying. I couldn't attend her going away party. I couldn't stop crying. Years later they moved back and I was ecstatic! We plan on going into the "ole folks' home" together. We really were sisters years ago. Thank goodness she's promised not to leave Georgia ever again.

Over twenty years ago three of us women wandered into each other and have been friends ever since, calling ourselves "the three amigos." Marka and Linda and I get together on a regular basis for lunch. We always laugh and cry and laugh some more. We joke that we have to stay friends forever because we know too much about each other. That's so true. We have an annual Christmas celebration, but sometimes we don't get around to it until July, which only makes the gift giving more fun. By then the gifts have been wrapped for months and we've usually forgotten what we're giving, so it's all a surprise to everyone.

Friends understand that your dogs come first. Friends

understand when you want to spit at your husband but love him dearly anyway. Friends understand your female problems. Friends are there when you go to the hospital, with a nice new set of pretty jammies for you to wear. Friends buy your lunch when you are broke. Friends listen to your troubles and then dismiss them when you do. Sometimes friends cry with you, but most of all they make you laugh and let you know you are loved.

We all need friends.

44. **No Braggin' Here** | 2015

Not only is Rick Bragg my favorite Southern writer, a favorite of thousands of readers, and the winner of the Pulitzer Prize, he is a genuine Southern gentleman to boot. Recently I learned this first hand.

Rick was on a book tour and came to Duluth, Georgia, to do a talk and signing at the Red Clay Theatre, which is right down the road from my house. The book was the biography *Jerry Lee Lewis: His Own Story.*

My husband, Richard, wasn't interested in going, so he dropped me off and I would call him to pick me up when it was over. I went inside the theatre to find a packed house.

Rick, as usual, was charming, interesting, and fun. After his talk about the book, he started answering questions. Eventually somebody asked about Jerry's child bride and Rick didn't quite know the full story. I stood up and said, "I know the answer to that question," and explained who I was and told them what they wanted to know. More questions came my way.

Rick was generous and didn't seem bothered at all that I was getting a bit of attention from his audience. I felt rather shy about it, but we ended up having a great discussion and I think everybody had a good time.

When it was over Rick started signing books and as I made my way through the crowd to leave I was surprised that people stopped me to sign the book, too. Again, Rick didn't seem to mind, so I obliged. I signed a lot of books and was so flattered that folks wanted my signature in that one.

I was there signing away until the very end. The lobby had finally cleared and I stepped outside to call Richard to come and get me. Before I could dial my phone, Rick stepped up beside me and asked if I needed a ride. He had a driver and they could drop me off. How thoughtful. I accepted and we had a lovely chat on the short ride to my house.

I've always admired his work. I'd heard great things about him from Phoebe, who was the one who'd initially worked with him to set up the writing of Jerry's biography. Now I had first-hand experience with the man and found him to be just as nice as it would seem.

Of course, I bought a copy of the book, signed by the author, and was curious to dig in to see what could possibly be in this book about Jerry Lee that hadn't already been covered in previous books about him. As always, Rick's writing was flawless. The book quickly became a best-seller. But... as I started to read I repeatedly found myself saying, "That isn't the way it was!" I knew right away what had happened. Rick had written what he was told. As usual, however, Jerry had told versions of his life events that he wanted people to believe, not always what had actually happened.

I couldn't finish the book.

It wasn't long before another book of Rick's came out, *My Southern Journey: True Stories of the South.* He came to my area to talk about that one, too, and once again I went and got a copy. Now that is a great book. I read it from cover to cover.

Rick Bragg's true stories are worth reading.

45. **Questions about Jerry** | 2015

People still ask me about Jerry Lee Lewis. Mostly, they want to know what I think of him today.

I think of Jerry Lee Lewis as seldom as possible.

Ha ha, all joking aside, there is no denying his amazing musical talent. I will always love his music.

But the man himself and I no longer have any kind of relationship.

Someone asked me recently how I *felt* about him now, after all these years.

Let me put it this way: How would you feel if for years you'd watched a person treat so badly the family that you love?

You've already read about how Jerry has never, to my knowledge, expressed appreciation to my daddy for getting him started in the music recording business. And he's never thanked either of my parents for the months of free room and board. (Cousin Mickey Gilley, by the way, has always been gracious to J.W. Brown for his support, even though Daddy got sick when they went to California and Daddy couldn't help Mickey very much.)

Jerry's treatment of me is another matter. I've been asked, more than once, if I think he was a cradle robber. Well, as I alluded to in an earlier chapter, it was a different era and people didn't necessarily think in those terms at that time, so I don't have an answer for that. But I do know that even back then if a twenty-two-year-old man wanted interesting conversation with a female, he wouldn't pick a thirteen-year-old girl. I was still jabbering about my arithmetic homework. If a twenty-two-year-old man, especially a rock-and-roller with a new hit record, wanted sex, he certainly wouldn't have any trouble finding it with some sexy babe of legal age. Let's face it: I was a cute kid but no Marilyn Monroe or Ann-Margret.

No, there's only one reason a twenty-two-year-old man would want to marry a child. He would want someone he could control. Someone he could mold the way he wanted. I doubt Jerry ever had that conscious thought—it's a pretty deep thought and deep thinking is not his forte—but I think that is what was going on. He joked about "raise 'em the way you want 'em" and I think that, without him even realizing it, that wasn't a joke for him. For a long time he did control me with verbal, emotional, and even physical abuse. In response, I did what immature girls do. I tried desperately to mold myself into what he wanted.

For a while. But then I grew up enough to realize that in good marriages nobody tries to control or mold anybody.

After all of these years, I still think about all of the times that J.L.L. slapped me, hit me, or shoved me. I never got to hit him back and I'm mad as hell about it. Just once I'd like to get a lick in on him.

But if you really want to know my deepest, darkest thoughts about Jerry Lee Lewis, let me tell you about his treatment of our daughter Phoebe. I know, I'm a mama bear with her hackles up when it comes to my child; now a brilliant, competent, beautiful, happy, grown woman. She doesn't need me to defend her. But I am her momma, after all. Like so many parents, maybe like you, I'll never stop protecting my child.

Eventually, as you've read by now, when the wives were all dead or had left him, and he was on too many prescription drugs, unhealthy, not performing, in enormous debt, and with no financial security for his future, Phoebe took the job as his manager and spent years getting him back in shape physically, financially, and professionally. She focused on getting her daddy well and back on stage, where he wanted to be. She got him off drugs. She got him slimmed down and eating healthy meals. She fixed his money woes, including paying off the IRS. She set up his first ever retirement fund. She hired a booking agent and got him on the road again, in moderation at his age, of course.

In other words, she saved his sorry ass.

In his most recent biography, Jerry never mentions any of this. Not even that she was the one who arranged the writing of that biography in the first place. His thanks to her was to make her life so miserable when he married his latest wife she had no alternative but to leave.

Never mind the fact that that wife was married to my brother at the time she and Jerry got together.

As you can see, I've not always been particularly fond of Jerry Lee Lewis.

My daddy is too much of a gentleman, my momma is too sweet, and my daughter loves her daddy too much to complain. I have no such constraints.

So, how do I *feel* about him?

I have resented him deeply.

At least, that's how I felt about Jerry Lee Lewis for long time.

But truth be told, I've mellowed over the years. A big part of that comes from my daughter, who continuously forgives her daddy for whatever thoughtless things he does. She says she understands him. She loves him, and she loves me. How Jerry Lee Lewis and I managed to have a child who grew up to be this smart and this kind I'll never know. But her forgiveness has helped me find a little of my own.

I've learned that holding anger in my heart does nothing but give that person I'm angry at control over my life. Why would I want to do that? I want to live my own life. Have I forgiven him? Yes, I must say that I have, somewhat. That didn't happen all at once like a lightning bolt had struck me with an electrifying epiphany. It happened little by little as I thought less and less about him and more and more about my own life and the people I love who are in it.

I'm not claiming to be a hundred percent there yet, but as time passes I get better and better at letting go of anger toward my ex-husband.

I've realized that forgiveness isn't for the other person, it's for yourself. You do it so that you can move on with your life, no longer giving that other person one iota of space in your thoughts or actions.

I suppose that for people who like to control others, that's hard to accept. If you're the one who's been manipulating others, driven them away, and still trying to yank their chain and they're just not even letting themselves be connected to that chain anymore, it would seem a rude awakening.

I have no idea if that kind of awakening has ever occurred to Jerry. Maybe he's mellowed with age, too.

I will say that he and I share a history together, good and bad, like one that few people ever experience. We had some deeply loving times together. We also had some deeply painful times. Best of all, we share a wonderful daughter who kept us connected for a number of years. But we've both moved on from any need to keep each other in our thoughts.

Jerry Lee Lewis is like a distant tune in the background of my life. I wish him no ill will. I truly hope he is happy.

I know I am.

46. **The Three Cousins** | 2015

In case you don't know the story of three of the Lewis cousins being famous—or infamous at times—here's a bit about the careers of Mickey Leroy Gilley, Jimmy Lee Swaggart, and Jerry Lee Lewis. All three are about the same age and grew up in or near the family hometown of Ferriday, Louisiana. It was natural that they were best friends since childhood.

Their grandparents were Arilla and Lee Lewis, my great-grandparents that I wrote about in the second chapter. The parents of these boys were siblings, three of the eleven children from that family. My daddy is also a cousin to these three boys, his mother being another of the eleven children. But Daddy is seven or eight years older than these three, so he didn't hang out with them when they were kids.

These three boys; Mickey, Jimmy, and Jerry; spent their Saturday afternoons watching whatever movie came to town, but westerns were their favorites. Horror pictures were a close second.

And they all loved music. As kids, they played the piano together, using the only piano around, one owned by the Swaggarts. They sang boogie-woogie and gospel, and Jerry and Jimmy loved sneaking away on Saturday nights to spy on Haney's Big House, the black juke joint in Ferriday.

They'd come home and try to imitate that rowdy sound like nothing they'd ever heard before. They certainly hadn't heard it in their little hometown church.

Jerry Lee wanted his own piano so badly that his dad, Elmo, in an effort to make the kid like him, worked hard to get it. You see, Elmo had missed the formative years of his son's life, having been in prison for bootlegging. Consequently, Jerry and his mom, Mamie, became very close. When Elmo returned, it was not to a warm welcome from either of them. From then on, Elmo seemed to live in his own prison in that household. However, in the end it was Aunt Stella Calhoun who gave Jerry Lee his first piano. That certainly paid off.

The fact that all three cousins; Mickey, Jimmy, and Jerry; reached enormous fame and success truly is astounding. These were three boys from a one horse town, not well educated—even as an adult Jerry never liked to read anything but comic books—and with no money, especially when Jimmy and Jerry's daddies both tangled with the law and spent time in jail for bootlegging. Each of those three boys clawed his way to the top of his chosen career.

Mickey Gilley garnered fame and fortune through country and pop music. Over a long singing and piano playing career, he had seventeen number one hits on the country charts. The use of his songs in the John Travolta film *Urban Cowboy* brought him even more recognition amongst fans worldwide. Apparently an astute businessman, he opened honky-tonk clubs that became wildly popular, and still owns Gilley's theater in Branson, Missouri. As of this writing, he is seventy-nine years old.

Jimmy Swaggart is a Pentecostal televangelist, gospel recording artist, and Christian book author. He started his preaching from the back of a borrowed flatbed truck. It's ironic that when Jerry hit it big first, he bought his cousin Jimmy an Oldsmobile so he'd have his own car for doing

God's work. Jimmy would drive that car around the countryside to preach. What some people were calling "the devil's music," rock-and-roll, made possible the spreading of the gospel. Jimmy went on to build a televangelism empire. He was thrown off his high pulpit many years ago because of a couple of hooker incidents, but he bounced back. He's a Lewis, after all. Music is a big part of his services and of his appeal. He's recorded and won numerous awards for his gospel music. Today his TV services are seen in over a hundred countries around the world. He is eighty years old.

And, as you know, Jerry Lee Lewis found his fame in rock-and-roll and eventually in country music, too. In 2015 he celebrated his eightieth birthday by performing to a huge crowd in England.

You have to admit, no matter what else has gone on in this family, those three have given the world a lot of joy and a lot to talk about. I often wonder what their grandmother Arilla Lewis would think of her grandsons. She lived long enough to see them rise to fame but not long enough to see all of the ups and downs. I suspect she's looking down from Heaven and shaking her head but smiling with pride all the same.

In fact, I think she loves us all—the good, the bad, and the in-between. That's the kind of woman she was—an inspiration to every Lewis and to anyone else who hears her story.

47. **Rekindling the Spark** | Today and Beyond

If my world ended tomorrow, I would insist that my life has been incredibly wonderful. Not every second of it, but just enough bad to make me enjoy the good so much more.

Enough good to make me feel as if I am the most fortunate person alive.

I don't live with regrets; I live with memories. I don't hold onto the pain of loss; I hold onto the memory of the love I have known.

As German philosopher Nietzsche said, "That which does not kill us, makes us stronger."

If I had been told before I was born that I would come into this world and would know many heartaches but would also have a beautiful, blue-eyed daughter that loved me like I love her, I would have said, "Okay, let's go! Let's do it!"

If I had known how powerful words are, how destructive and damaging to the soul they can be, I would have stuffed cotton in my ears and sung "lalalalalalalalala" real loud for a long time.

That's why writing my words, my life story, here has meant so much to me. I hope that my words in some way have the power to help heal the soul—yours and mine. I hope that my words make you want to sing with joy and dance in the light of your own spark that has survived. If I could survive, so can you.

When I look back at what I have accomplished in my life, I think about my great-grandmother Arilla Lewis. So often I've asked myself, "What would she have done?" My guess is that she would have done the exact same things that I have done, and that makes me feel good. She had to be a tower of strength. I believe she instilled that strength in her future generations because she somehow knew we would need it.

My gift to you is a continuation of that strength. From Arilla to me, and from me to you. Ignite that spark in you and let it shine!

PHOTOGRAPHS

Myra Gale Brown, about age 3

Newlyweds Jerry Lee Lewis & Myra, 1957

Jerry Lee and Myra on the fateful
trip to England, 1958.
They made the French newspapers, too.

LE DRAME commence à la douane anglaise. Myra, la femme de Jerry Lewis avait menti avant gagner une Scandale : elle n'a

The couple during happy times.

top: Jerry Lee and Myra
left: J.W. Brown and his brother Otis, who played fiddle with the Mississippi Hotshots. Otis was in General Patton's division in World War II.
right: J.W. and Lois Brown in the 1950s

J.W. Brown in Australia. Photo taken by Paul Anka

Jerry Lee, drummer Russ, and J.W. Brown. Picture taken by Buddy Holly on
Australian tour. Courtesy Graham Knight, Hali Chelette.

J.W. Brown on Jerry Lee's DC-3 plane.

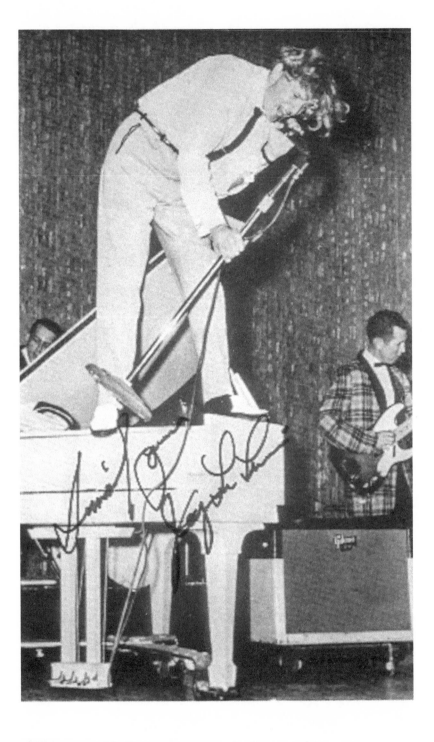

above: A scene from *High School Confidential*

left: Jerry Lee and J.W. Brown. At Ellis Auditorium, Memphis. That amplifier accidentally caught on fire. J.W. kicked it to the side of the stage and great balls of fire became a part of the act.

below: Russ, J.W., and Jerry Lee in a scene from the movie *Jamboree*

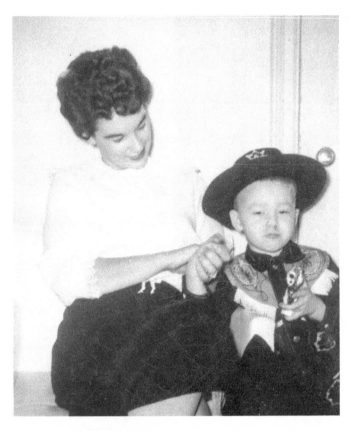

Lois & Rusty Brown, 1957

left: J.W. and Lois Brown in Atlanta. *right:* J.W. Brown, 1970

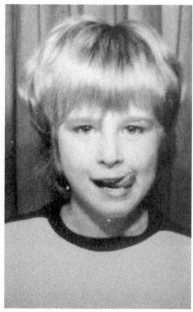

Phoebe Lewis at age 3 (left) and about age 5 (right)

Jerry Lee and Phoebe at her 5th birthday party

Phoebe Lewis

Phoebe Lewis
with her father,
Jerry Lee Lewis

Phoebe used to donate her hair to make wigs for children who had cancer.

Phoebe and her husband Ezekiel Asa Loftin XII, 2013.
He's the founder of *Twisted South Magazine.*

Phoebe, 2015

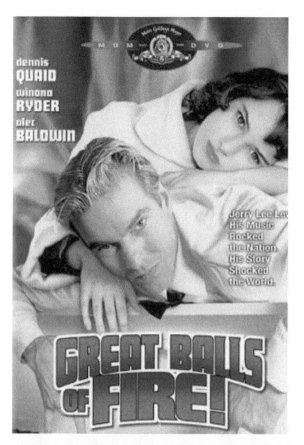

top: The movie based on Myra's book. *above left:* The family with the actors JoÚ Doe, Lisa Blount, and Winona Ryder. *above right:* Myra's book, *Great Balls of Fire,* 1988

RAH RAH REAL ESTATE

This is what I do now!

IM PROUD TO BE A ~~REELTOR~~ ~~REALATER~~ ~~REALADDER~~ REALTOR

YOU SHOW MINE AND I'LL SHOW YOURS

"A Realtor With a Past"

Myra Williams
Broker Associate

"Powerhouse" founder and chairperson since 1988. Powerhouse is a network of Realtors knowledgeable in the "Executive Price Range". Homes that truly "go beyond the ordinary" and a Realtor that will go beyond the expected.

Almost 2 decades of experience, as a broker, a certified appraiser and a multi million dollar producer.

However, the bottom line is...it's not about my credentials, it's about you... it's not about my needs...it's about yours.

Consulting
Researching
Evaluating
Negotiating
Managing the Details
Specialized Service as a Buyer's Representative

When you make the biggest investment of your life, wouldn't it be nice to have someone on your side, *someone with a past.*

2000

Child bride of rock 'n' roll legend speaks ou

By J. KRISTIN STULTZ
Special to the Citizen

Before the Beatles, before the Beach Boys, before the Rolling Stones, there was Jerry Lee Lewis. And before Jerry Lee Lewis set the world's spotlight on rock 'n' roll, he married his 13-year-old second cousin, Myra Brown. Their marriage, like Lewis' music, had the whole world shook up.

Now divorced from Lewis and married to a Gwinnett County man, Myra Lewis Williams and her husband, Richard, live in Duluth and work in Lawrenceville, where Richard Williams is the broker in charge of a real estate agency and Myra Williams is an agent. Although she is happy with the quiet life she's led with Williams since their 1984 wedding, she will never forget the 13 years she lived and loved with first husband Jerry Lee Lewis.

Myra Lewis Williams – whose controversial marriage to Jerry Lee Lewis rocked the music scene in the 1950s – now calls Duluth home and says she and her piano-playing ex-husband are friends. –Special photo

published in 1982)," she said, "I went back and asked him when was the first time he felt like he loved me, and he said – 'Girl,' as he affectionately called me, 'I loved you the

live or now or never. I took now, and the next afternoon, we got in the car and drove to Wallace, Miss., and the preacher married us. We told my mother and daddy that we

was married to this little girl," Williams said. "One of the reporters (at the London airport) came to me and asked me who I was, and I said, 'I'm Jerry's wife,' and he said,

really think that it w supposed to happen. I was fated."

When Lewis's caree took a turn for the wo his home life became much better. In 1959, son, Steve Allen Lewi was born. Myra was n happier, and Jerry wa working as hard as ev Even though he hadn had a hit for several months, the Lewis ho was built on solid gro While Jerry kept tryi break into the music ness again, Myra care their son. Together, th fought the world that turned against them. enough, they had to fi another loss together. Young "Stevie," as he called, drowned in 19 Before her 20th birth Myra Williams had se her husband lose his career and their son b his life. It was almost more than she could stand.

Still in intense grie Lewises welcomed the daughter, Phoebe, in Finally, Myra had ma

Richard Williams, real estate agency owner and broker

Richard Williams

above: Richard Williams with his father Harper, his son Brookie, and his daughter Hilah.

right: golfer Richard Williams

Myra planting a hosta at Steve's grave.

Myra in Winnsboro, LA, where her daddy once slept in an alley

Cousins Mickey Gilley, Jimmy Swaggart, and Jerry Lee Lewis

left: Cousins Mickey Gilley and J.W. Brown, 2000
right: Cousin Jimmy Swaggart

J.W. Brown and his Fender bass, Memphis Rock & Soul Museum,
between Jerry Lee and Elvis

J.W. and his Fender bass

Rusty and J.W. Brown

Phoebe, Jerry Lee, and Myra, early 2000s

The Three Amigos: Marka Palmer, Myra Lewis Williams, and Linda Hughes

J.W. and Rusty Brown's book, 2010

Myra with publishers Jan and Bob Babcock of Deeds Publishing, and fellow writers Marka Palmer and Linda Hughes for the launch of the book *Atlanta's Real Women*, 2013

Some of the writers for *What We Talk about When We're Over 60:* Mary Mattson, Linda Hughes, Myra Lewis Williams, Kathryn Gray-White, and Brenda Cox, 2014

left: Myra at book signing, 2014
right: Myra and writer Rick Bragg, 2015

Myra with photographer Jim Herrington, 2016

Myra and Richard

ABOUT THE AUTHOR

My first book, *Great Balls of Fire*, published in 1989, turned out to be a publisher's idea of the only part of my life he thought anyone would be interested in: my marriage at age thirteen to my second-cousin Jerry Lee Lewis. The movie by the same name ended up being a producer's idea of how he thought my life should have been. Never before has my real life story been told. Well, this is it. I've finally been able to write my story in my own words. I hope you find it to be inspiring and helpful. Or at the very least, I hope it gives you some chuckles along the way. Thank you so much for reading *The Spark that Survived*. My best wishes to you in fanning the flames of your own life story.

Visit Myra's website at www.myralewiswilliams.com
Join her on Facebook at
www.facebook.com/myralewiswilliamsauthor

CPSIA information can be obtained
at www.ICGtesting.com
Printed in the USA
BVHW032001120421
604754BV00006B/240